GW00361615

Watching Wildlife in Suffolk

A guide to Suffolk Wildlife Trust nature reserves

Edited by Audrey Boyle with design by Peter Cockburn

Published in the UK May 2001 by Suffolk Wildlife Trust
Brooke House, Ashbocking, Ipswich, Suffolk IP6 9JY

Registered charity no. 262777

© Copyright Suffolk Wildlife Trust 2001.

ISBN 0901 588075

Production and copy editor: Audrey Boyle
Text: Audrey Boyle and Christine Luxton
Design and cartography: Peter Cockburn with The Five Castles Press
Photography and front cover: David Hosking
Additional photos: T. Andrewartha, S. Aylward,
R. Chittenden, C. Jakes, D. Jones and M. J. Thomas
Illustrations: Bill Stevenson
Leaf beetle illustration based on original by John Read
Printing: The Five Castles Press, Ipswich, Suffolk
Front Cover: Dingle Marshes

FOREWORD

SUFFOLK HAS IT ALL – heathlands and coastlands, woods and meadows. This great variety provides homes for a huge range of animals and plants, some common, others rare and a few that are being specially protected for they are endangered.

This guide will be invaluable to everyone who wants to explore the county's riches. Spending time in wild places and learning about the natural world is one of the greatest joys.

By buying this guide you will not only be enhancing your pleasure, you will also be helping to give Suffolk's wildlife a more secure future.

Sir David Attenborough

ACKNOWLEDGEMENTS

SUFFOLK WILDLIFE TRUST would like to thank the voluntary reserve wardens who help care for these special sites and who provided much of the information included in this book and SWT field officers who patiently checked and double-checked the wildlife facts and practical details.

Photographer David Hosking went out of his way to meet the brief in what was a tight schedule and rose to the challenge of providing superb shots despite the vagaries of our British summer. Artist Bill Stevenson gave freely of his time, producing drawings of the more obscure species in next to no time, and Five Castles Press provided advice on tap and pulled out all the stops when it came to final printing. We are grateful to them all. Without their help this book could not have been produced.

David Hosking would like to thank field staff and reserve wardens for taking time to show him around and point out special features and wildlife. Lindacre Land Rover of Ipswich kindly provided David with the use of a four-wheel drive vehicle capable of negotiating the more remote tracks, when he was temporarily without a car. That he won't forget!

Finally the Trust would like to thank the landowners with whom we have leases and management agreements. Their co-operation and support is vital in ensuring that the Trust can manage these areas for their wildlife, first and foremost.

We are also grateful to the Environment Agency who assisted with the production costs of this book.

ABOUT SUFFOLK WILDLIFE TRUST

S UFFOLK WILDLIFE TRUST, a charity set up in 1961, is one of a national network of 46 Wildlife Trusts and aims to protect and conserve the wildlife and habitats of Suffolk for the future.

A large membership gives us influence and helps us make a real difference. We believe that wildlife is essential to a healthy environment for people and we work with those from all walks of life – families, communities, landowners, industry and local and central government – to make sure nature has a fighting chance. *This includes:*

- caring for 62 nature reserves including those featured in this handbook along with many other sites
- campaigning at a local and national level on wildlife issues
- monitoring local planning applications and commenting on development plans
- advising landowners, farmers and industry on how to manage their land for wildlife
- involving people in nature conservation – we run over 300 practical work parties each year
- holding walks, talks and events in your area through a network of local groups
- recording sites of wildlife value – so far we have identified over 800 County Wildlife Sites and 100 roadside nature reserves
- working with local communities to enable people to take action for wildlife on their own doorstep
- reaching out to schools with the wildlife message
- making wildlife fun and accessible for all!

Your support is vital to the survival of Suffolk's wildlife.

To find out more about how you can help please contact **Suffolk Wildlife Trust, Brooke House, Ashbocking, Ipswich IP6 9JY. Telephone: 01473 890089.**

Or visit our website at **www.wildlifetrust.org.uk/suffolk**

ABOUT THIS GUIDE

Welcome!

We hope you enjoy getting out and about with
Suffolk Wildlife Trust's new reserves guide and
discovering just how fantastic Suffolk's wildlife is.
Whether it's on your doorstep, in town or hidden
away in traditional countryside, there's a whole
host of weird, wonderful and fascinating animals,
plants and places to explore.

Arranged in alphabetical order (apart from four
smaller sites which appear at the back),
information on the 55 reserves selected for this
book is designed to give you a flavour of what to
expect – we think the quote at the beginning
captures the 'feel' of each. We can't include
everything, but hopefully provide a colourful
sketch of every reserve.

*Making wildlife fun! Adult
courses and children's activitie
run throughout the year at the
Trust's education centres*

The star species highlighted are wildlife for
which the site is special and which you as
a visitor stand a reasonable chance of seeing.
Specially commissioned photographs by local and
internationally acclaimed wildlife photographer
David Hosking and drawings by Suffolk artist
Bill Stevenson are designed to whet your appetite
by providing a taster of each.

Generally each reserve is freely accessible unless
otherwise stated. Occasionally though, it *is* necessary
to restrict access to protect sensitive or breeding
wildlife, and we ask you to take note of our requests
regarding dogs.

Each reserve featured is a valuable wildlife habitat in its
own right, but some may be extra special being the
only refuge in Suffolk, or even Britain, for some species.
Consequently the status of each site is provided –
abbreviations are included in the key overleaf.

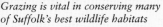
Grazing is vital in conserving many of Suffolk's best wildlife habitats

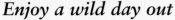

Enjoy a wild day out

To find your chosen reserve we suggest you arm yourself with an up-to-date Ordnance Survey map. We've provided detailed grid references and drawn up location and site maps intended for use alongside your OS map, so hopefully you can't go wrong! Parking, the closest location for cafes and pubs and details of wheelchair and pushchair access are also provided to ensure the whole family can enjoy a day out together.

Many sites are accessible by public transport and visitors are urged to use this where possible in order to reduce environmental impact. Train and bus times can be obtained by contacting Suffolk County Council's Suffolk Traveline on 08459 583358 (local rates apply) or national Traveline on 0870 6082608.

Although most of our reserves are worth a visit at almost any time of year, we have indicated the very best months to make it easier to choose where to go and when. In cases when there is another Trust reserve nearby – usually within around five miles (9km) – we've listed that too for easy reference. Why not make a day of it? Now the only thing left to do is for you to get out there, explore and ENJOY!

Volunteering with one of the Trust's teams is a great way of getting to know the county and its wildlife

RESERVES MAP

(v) visitor or education centre

* *opens 2002*

RESERVES MAP

Suffolk Wildlife Trust

Brooke House
Ashbocking
Suffolk
IP6 9JY
Tel: 01473 890089

Thank you

Thank you for deciding to support Suffolk Wildlife Trust as a Benefactor member with your donation of £ 5 per month / year. Your Account will be debited monthly/annually.

The above amount will be requested from your bank on approximately the 25th of each month.

Welcome

We would like to welcome you to Suffolk Wildlife Trust. If you have any queries about your membership please contact our Membership Co-ordinator, Caroline Sherrod on: 01473 890089

Your membership pack will introduce you to the Trust's work. You can also find out more on our website www.suffolkwildlife.co.uk

The Direct Debit Guarantee

This Guarantee is offered by all Banks and Building Societies that take part in the Direct Debit Scheme. The efficiency and security of the Scheme is monitored and protected by your own Bank or Building Society.

If the payment dates change, you will be told of this in advanced by at least 14 days as agreed.

If an error is made by Suffolk Wildlife Trust or your bank or Building Society, you are guaranteed a full and immediate refund from your branch of the amount paid.

You can cancel a Direct Debit at any time by writing to your Bank or Building Society. Please also send a copy of your letter to us at Suffolk Wildlife Trust, Brooke House, Ashbocking, Suffolk IP6 9JY

We will keep your details on our secure database to enable us to send you magazines and other information about Suffolk Wildlife Trust or The Wildlife Trusts.

We value your support and do not pass on information about Trust members to any group or individual outside The Wildlife Trusts.

If you would like to restrict the information we send you, please let us know.

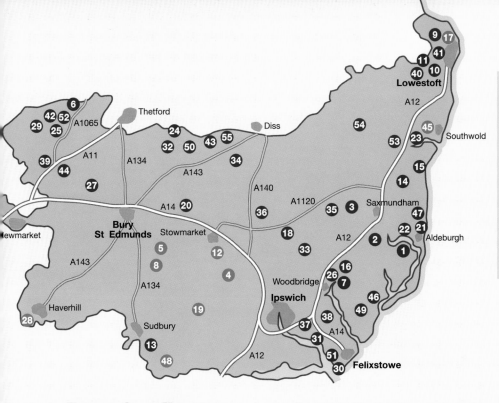

Reserves Status Key

CWS – County Wildlife Site
A site of county wildlife importance identified by Suffolk Wildlife Trust and Suffolk County Council.

LNR – Local Nature Reserve
Sites of local importance for wildlife where there are opportunities for the public to learn about and enjoy wildlife. Established by local authorities and English Nature.

Natura 2000 site
Sites of European importance which host priority habitat types or priority species which are particularly at risk.

NNR – *National Nature Reserve*
National designation by English Nature for some of the UK's finest wildlife sites.

Ramsar Sites
Sites of international importance for wetland birds designated under the Ramsar convention.

SSSI – *Site of Special Scientific Interest*
A site of national importance identified by English Nature for its ecological or geological value.

ALDE MUDFLATS

"Bright, icy winter mornings; plaintive calls of wigeon and the shrill of literally hundreds of dunlin make it a favourite."

Winter is the best time to view Alde Mudflats when impressive numbers of black-tailed godwit and striking black and white avocet can be seen strutting and probing the gloopy 'ooze' for succulent titbits.
Make sure you time your visit when the tide is out so the vast expanses of mudflat, harbouring lavish feasts of invertebrates, are fully exposed.

The lack of access on this protected site ensures birds have an undisturbed sanctuary for feeding and roosting. Large numbers of dunlin, curlew, black-tailed godwit, oystercatcher, grey plover, wigeon, pintail and teal also use the reserve in winter. During the breeding season redshank, avocet and oystercatcher raise their young here with majestic marsh harrier nesting close by.

For the best views arm yourself with binoculars (and a hot flask in winter) and take the footpath from Iken Cliff car park eastwards towards Iken Church. There are also good views from the bird-hide at Hazelwood reserve on the other side of the estuary.

Alde Mudflats are leased by Suffolk Wildlife Trust from the Crown Estate.

Other Trust reserves nearby: Blaxhall Common

STAR SPECIES
Avocet
Black-tailed godwit

Elegant avocet are easily spotted with their black and white plumage and long blue legs

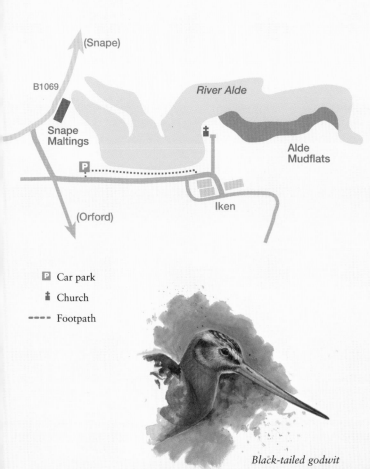

(Snape)

B1069

Snape
Maltings

River Alde

✝

Alde
Mudflats

P

Iken

(Orford)

P Car park

✝ Church

- - - - Footpath

Black-tailed godwit

Map
OS Landranger 156

Grid reference
TM 420570

Size
122 hectares (305 acres)

Status
SSSI, Natura 2000

Parking
Iken Cliff car park

Local facilities
Snape Maltings

Access
None, but can be viewed
from river or Iken Cliff
footpath west of church

Best time to visit
Nov–March

BLAXHALL COMMON

"The hypnotic hum of insects on a summer's day gives way to the strange churring of one of our most enigmatic summer visiting birds, the nightjar, as the sun sinks."

The calming, insular feel of this heathland is hard to describe. It holds an attraction for wildlife too and birds like woodlark, nightjar, goldcrest, long-tailed tit and tree pipit can be found alongside common lizard, adder and plants like heath milkwort, speedwell, heath bedstraw and sheep's sorrel.

In summer small copper, common blue and small heath butterflies dance in the clearings while the bold red and white fly agaric, a poisonous mushroom so often portrayed in children's fairytales, is among the many fungi that appear, as if by magic, in autumn.

The peaceful common is small but full of surprises like winter visiting crossbill and colonies of ant-lion. The site is looked after by seasonal cutting which controls invasive scrub and maintains the medley of habitats.

Blaxhall Common is cared for by Suffolk Wildlife Trust on behalf of Blaxhall Parish Council.

Other Trust reserves nearby: Alde Mudflats

STAR SPECIES
Woodlark

Nightjar

Adder

Ant-lion

Straight out of a fairy tale – the fly agaric mushroom

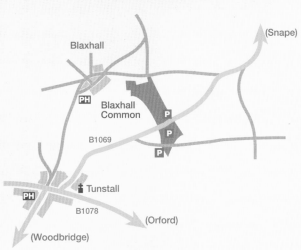

Blaxhall

PH

Blaxhall
Common

B1069

P

P

P

(Snape)

i Tunstall

PH

B1078

(Orford)

(Woodbridge)

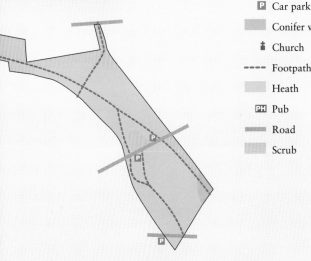

P Car park

Conifer woodland

i Church

---- Footpath

Heath

PH Pub

Road

Scrub

P

P

P

Map
OS Landranger 156

Grid reference
TM 382564

Size
44 hectares (110 acres)

Status
SSSI

Parking
Small car parks off the
B1069 and Iken road

Local facilities
Blaxhall, Tunstall, Snape

Walking conditions
Dry & firm

Dogs
Under control please

Best time to visit
May–Sept

*On warm days the shy adder
basks in secluded spots*

BONNY WOOD

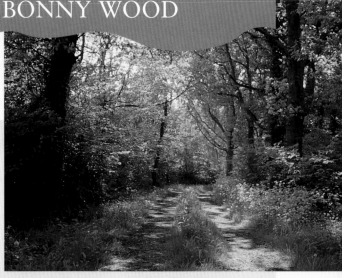

"A fantastic ancient, semi-natural woodland with superb circular walks. During spring it's worth getting here for the dawn chorus alone!"

Bonny Wood lies about half a mile from Barking Tye, and is a Site of Special Scientific Interest for the sheer quality of its habitats. The best time to visit is from late April to late June when the coppiced areas are brimming with plants like wood anemone, woodruff and herb-paris. There are also patches of wild garlic, twayblade and early-purple orchid. If you look carefully, you may spot greater butterfly orchid.

Birds are plentiful with melodies from summer migrants such as nightingale, blackcap and willow warbler mingling with the song of resident species. The larger trees are used by tawny owl, treecreeper and all three species of woodpecker. There are frequent sightings of hobby and at dusk you may snatch a glimpse of woodcock performing their mating display. Evidence of a healthy badger population is reflected by the number of setts.

This site's recorded history dates back to 1251. In 1561 Elizabeth I bought the woods from the Bishop of Ely. Later in 1611, the property was sold by King James I and eventually passed to the Ashburnham Estate, who harvested the wood on a regular basis for hop poles, thatching, hurdles, tool handles and firewood.

Greater butterfly orchid

STAR SPECIES

Badger

Herb-paris

Badger are most active at night

Since Suffolk Wildlife Trust purchased the wood in 1987, the traditional management of coppicing has been re-introduced. The rides are cut to create sunny areas for butterflies and flowering plants.

Other Trust reserves nearby: Combs Wood

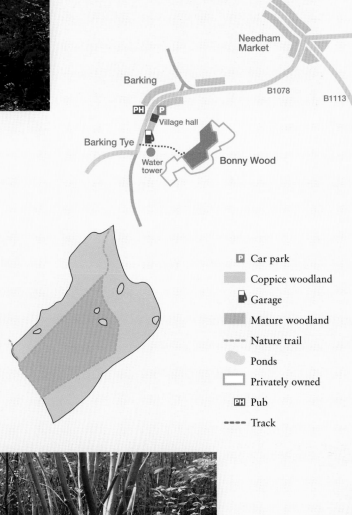

Needham Market

Barking

B1078

B1113

PH P

Village hall

Barking Tye

Water tower

Bonny Wood

P Car park

Coppice woodland

Garage

Mature woodland

--- Nature trail

Ponds

Privately owned

PH Pub

---- Track

Map
OS Landranger 155

Grid reference
TM 076520

Size
20 hectares (50 acres)

Status
SSSI

Parking
Local hall

Local facilities
Local pub

Walking conditions
Often wet and sticky

Dogs
On leads only

Best time to visit
April–June

Coppicing prolongs a tree's life

BRADFIELD WOODS

"This National Nature Reserve is one of the UK's best woodland wildlife sites. The revival of traditional crafts like charcoal production and hurdle making has ensured it remains a tremendous magnet for wildlife."

Bradfield Woods National Nature Reserve is a working wood that has been under continuous traditional management since 1252, supplying local needs for firewood and hazel products. One of Britain's finest ancient woodlands the site is a glorious haven for wildlife. The range in soil types from acid to alkaline explains the impressive variety of plants – 370 at the last count!

Look out for colourful flushes of spring flowers in the newly coppiced areas. April is the best time to visit to see early-purple orchid and wood anemone growing alongside nationally rare oxlip. As the coppice shoots regenerate, their dense bushy growth provides cover for migrant songbirds such as garden warbler, blackcap and enigmatic nightingale whose delightful song alone makes this reserve worth a visit. Mammals including the yellow-necked mouse, secretive dormouse and nocturnal badger are also resident.

STAR SPECIES
Oxlip
Nightingale
Roe deer

On sunny summer days the sheltered rides harbour breath-taking clouds of butterflies, of which there are 24 species.

Guelder rose berries provide a winter feast for many birds

*Hazel coppice provides food
and shelter for secretive dormice*

Nightingale

*Coppiced wood
products from Bradfield
are still used for thatching,
tool handles, rustic poles,
hurdle-making and firewood*

*The ringlet butterfly soaks up
the sun in clearings and rides*

The traditional management of coppicing at Bradfield
involves cutting the stems and allowing the trees
to re-grow before they are cut again some 20-25 years later.
Coppiced stems are used for firewood, fencing and
thatching spars. Some trees have been allowed to grow
into mature specimens to provide larger timber. Trees and
shrubs growing here include oak, ash, alder, hazel, maple,
small-leaved lime, dogwood and spindle. Old oak and ash
pollards line the east and south boundary.

If you visit the reserve in early morning keep quiet and you
may be lucky enough to see deer picking their way daintily
along the rides. Medium sized roe deer are the most
common but the larger red deer and spotted fallow also
occur. The tiny dog-sized muntjac deer is spotted regularly
in the woods.

The best way to enjoy this site is to explore the many rides.
Pick up a trail guide at the visitor centre when you arrive.

Please note that Bradfield Woods is referred to as Felshamhall
Wood on the OS map.

Other Trust reserves nearby: Bulls Wood

*Wild angelica favours damp,
shady places*

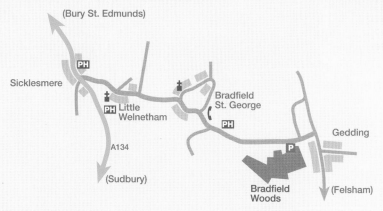

(Bury St. Edmunds)

Sicklesmere

Little Welnetham

A134

(Sudbury)

Bradfield St. George

Gedding

PH

P

Bradfield Woods

(Felsham)

P   Car park

     Coppice woodland

■   Hide

---- Nature trails

     Mature woodland

     Privately owned

PH Pub

---- Public footpath

(Telephone

     Visitor centre

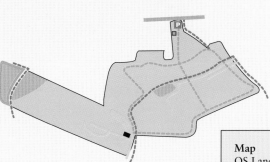

Small, slender roe deer are often spotted by the woodland's edge

Map
OS Landranger 155

Grid reference
TL 935581

Size
72 hectares (180 acres)

Status
NNR, visitor centre
(no loos)

Parking
At reserve entrance

Local facilities
Local pubs

Walking conditions
Often wet and sticky

Dogs
On leads only

Wheelchair/pushchair
Accessible in parts

Best time to visit
April–Oct, Jan

BROMESWELL GREEN

"Small but charming with a bit of everything from river habitat to woodland and wet meadow."

Bromeswell Green is noted for its wet meadows, saltmarsh and woodland. Wetland plants such as southern marsh orchid, lesser spearwort and fen bedstraw make a wonderful display in the damper areas, while climbing corydalis is more typical of the drier parts. Common lizard can be seen basking on warm sunny days.

This reserve is part of the Deben Estuary SSSI. At low tide, the river attracts hordes of feeding waders including redshank and greenshank. Look out too for the iridescent flashes of kingfisher along the banks.

The woodland supports many summer visiting birds like nightingale, whitethroat and blackcap. Plaintive cascading song from the willow warbler can be heard April to June. In winter redpoll and siskin feed on alder seeds in the woods. Rides are mown annually to provide ideal conditions for the numerous species of butterfly.

STAR SPECIES

Kingfisher

Southern marsh orchid

Common lizard absorb most of their energy from the sun

Although part of the reserve is owned by Suffolk Wildlife Trust, most of Bromeswell Green is cared for by the Trust on behalf of Bromeswell Parish Council. The meadows are usually cut, raked and then grazed by sheep to conserve the variety of plants and flowers.

Other Trust reserves nearby: Foxburrow Farm, Hutchison's Meadow, Sutton and Hollesley Commons

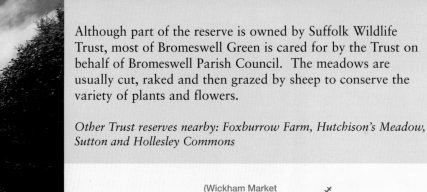

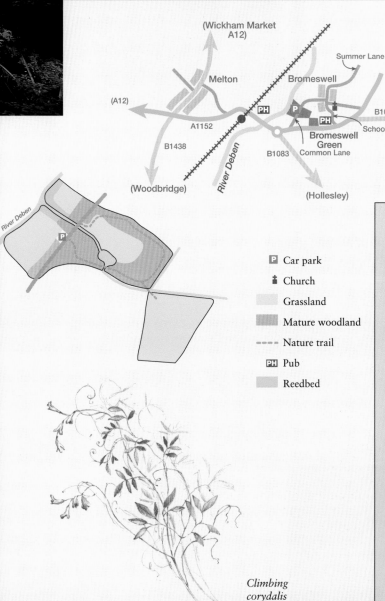

P Car park

✝ Church

Grassland

Mature woodland

---- Nature trail

PH Pub

Reedbed

Map
OS Landranger 156

Grid reference
TM 296504

Size
7.2 hectares (18 acres)

Status
CWS, SSSI

Parking
Down Common Lane alongside reserve

Local facilities
Local pubs

Walking conditions
Muddy in places

Dogs
On leads only as grazing stock

Best time to visit
May–July

Climbing corydalis

BULL'S WOOD

"So tranquil that it comes as a surprise to encounter another soul in these ancient woods."

This tranquil ancient woodland is the last fragment of the many woods of Cockfield, referred to in the Hundred Rolls of 1279. April is the best month to visit Bull's Wood which is famed for its oxlips – a delicate yellow flowered plant limited to 100 sites in East Anglia – which carpet parts of the woodland floor in spring. Early-purple orchid are abundant here and you'll see spurge-laurel, wood anemone and herb-paris – all uncommon plants associated with ancient woodland.

Birds include chiffchaff, treecreeper, tawny owl, marsh and long-tailed tit. Many of the rides have been opened up to create sunny, grassy glades enjoyed by butterflies such as ringlet, gatekeeper and orange tip.

The wood's long history of coppicing is being continued by local volunteers. This traditional method of harvesting wood creates a mosaic of wildlife habitats and encourages the spectacular show of spring flowers. The coppiced trees are mostly ash, hazel and field maple while the oaks are normally left to mature.

STAR SPECIES
Oxlip
Wood anemone

Other Trust reserves nearby:
Bradfield Woods

C. Jakes

Oxlip prefer chalky soils and coppice management

Dryad's saddle fungus is a parasite of deciduous trees

- P **Car park**
- ▨ **Coppice woodland**
- ⛪ **Church**
- ▥ **Mature woodland**
- - - - **Nature trail**
- ⬭ **Pond**
- PH **Pub**
- ---- **Public footpath**
- P **Roadside parking**
- ☏ **Telephone**
- ······· **Track**
- 🗼 **Windmill**

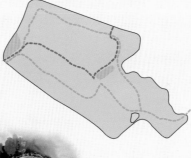

Map
OS Landranger 155

Grid reference
TL 925547

Size
11.7 hectares (29.25 acres)

Status
SSSI

Parking
Palmers Farm on concrete by walnut tree. Look for village sign at farm turning

Local facilities
Local pubs

Walking conditions
Wet in winter

Dogs
On leads only

Best time to visit
April

Tawny owl

CAMPS HEATH

"Ragged-robin in the sun, dragonflies hawking in their run, bogbean growing in a crowd, drifts of orchids standing proud ... "

This is a unique fen meadow with literally dozens of rare plants. In spring and summer, early and southern marsh orchid vie with marsh pea and bogbean for the flower lover's attention. Other plants like red bartsia, bog pimpernel, greater spearwort, marsh pennywort and ragged-robin can also be found.

Grass snake, with their distinctive yellow collar, and common lizard languish in sheltered sunny spots and rare freshwater snails are a speciality. In winter snipe and short-eared owls can be spotted searching out a meal.

STAR SPECIES

Early & Southern marsh orchid

Bogbean

This tranquil reserve is partly grazed with horses and cattle and partly mown, to conserve the diversity of its plants and other associated wildlife.

Camps Heath is cared for by Suffolk Wildlife Trust on behalf of Suffolk County Council. As this is not an open reserve please contact the Trust to request entry.

Other Trust reserves nearby: Carlton Marshes, Castle Marshes, Foxburrow Wood, North Cove, Oulton Marshes

Red bartsia

Ragged-robin

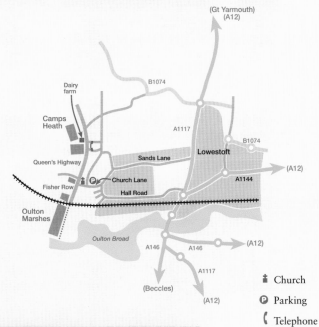

(Gt Yarmouth)
(A12)

B1074

Dairy
farm

Camps
Heath

A1117

Lowestoft

B1074

Queen's Highway

Sands Lane

(A12)

Fisher Row

Church Lane

A1144

Hall Road

Oulton
Marshes

Oulton Broad

A146

A146

(A12)

A1117

(Beccles)

(A12)

✝ Church

P Parking

☏ Telephone

Map
OS Landranger 134

Grid reference
TM 509943

Size
6.3 hectares (15.75 acres)

Status
CWS, Broads National Park

Parking
Along Church Lane by
Oulton Church

Local facilities
Oulton

Access
By permission only

Walking conditions
Wet, uneven ground

Dogs
Sorry no dogs

Best time to visit
April–July

*The short-eared owl's
sensitive hearing enables
it to detect prey on
the ground*

CARLTON MARSHES

*"It still retains its wild,
untamed character –
a magical marsh plain
with whispering
reeds under wide,
open skies."*

Carlton Marshes lies in the Waveney Valley at the southern
tip of the Norfolk and Suffolk Broads and comprises over
100 acres of grazing marsh, fens and peat pools.
It is the Broads in miniature. Flower studded marshes drained
by a system of dykes and grazed by cattle in summer,
create a paradise for wintering wading birds and birds of
prey including the hobby. Water vole may be seen in and
around the dykes along with special plants including the
rare and protected water soldier.

In early summer wet fen meadows around
Sprat's Water are bursting with ragged-robin,
southern marsh orchid, lesser
and greater spearwort and
bogbean. Both Sprat's and
Round Water are the result
of peat digging carried out
long ago.

STAR SPECIES

*Norfolk hawker
& Scarce chaser
dragonfly*

Water vole

Marsh harrier

Bladderwort

The open water in both these pools is heaving with life including insectivorous bladderwort. This unusual plant lives off unsuspecting water fleas which it traps and digests in bladder-like sacs under water.

Carlton Marshes is one of the best places in the UK for a range of freshwater snails which reflects the good water quality in the dykes. The reed and sedge beds along the river wall make ideal nesting cover for reed and sedge warblers, bearded tit, Cetti's warbler and marsh harrier. An astounding 15 kinds of dragonfly have been spotted here including the rare Norfolk hawker. A visit at dusk during summer may be rewarded with views of the magical glow-worm.

Norfolk hawker dragonfly

R. Chittenden

Mowing and cattle grazing are used by the Trust to conserve the fen meadow and marshland wildlife. Dykes are regularly cleared and mud pumping is vital in the pools to prevent them silting up. Activities for local schools and a range of family events are run from the well-equipped and friendly visitor centre.

Other Trust reserves nearby: Camps Heath, Castle Marshes, Foxburrow Wood, North Cove, Oulton Marshes

The water vole has suffered the most rapid, dramatic and serious decline of any British wild mammal

Bogbean

The male bearded tit with its eye-catching grey head and black moustache, feeds on insects in summer and seeds in winter

(Gt. Yarmouth)

A1117   A1144

Oulton Broad

A146

Carlton Marshes

P

PH Lowestoft

A1117

Burnt Hill Lane

(A12 South)

A146

(Beccles)

Oulton Broad

P

→ Brown sign to reserve

P Car park

Car showroom

— Dyke network

■ Education centre

Fen/grazing marsh

---- Nature trail

Petrol station

PH Pub

Reedbed

Wet woodland

Map
OS Landranger 134

Grid reference
TM 508921

Size
44.9 hectares (112.25 acres)

Status
Broads National Park, SSSI, Natura 2000, Education and visitor centre

Parking
At end of Burnt Hill Lane, Carlton Colville

Local facilities
Reserve visitor centre, Oulton Broad

Walking conditions
Good on hard paths, may be muddy in places

Dogs
On leads only

Wheelchair/pushchair
Access on hard paths and into centre

Best time to visit
May–July

CASTLE MARSHES

"A real dragonfly experience with a wealth of flowering aquatic plants and wading birds – what more can you ask for!"

Castle Marshes is a Broadland site with grazing marsh, fen and freshwater dykes. In winter the marshes are flooded to create expanses of open water for wintering wildfowl that swell the resident populations of wigeon, teal, shoveler and gadwall. Birds of prey like marsh harrier and hobby can often be seen quartering the marshes.

In and around the sparkling, unpolluted dykes dividing the marshes, plants like rare water soldier, frogbit and flowering rush hold forth. Norfolk hawker dragonfly – a national rarity which breeds here – can be seen hunting along the river wall between June and September, along with the blue-tailed damselfly and scarce chaser.

Water levels are kept high in spring to accommodate breeding lapwing and redshank. Traditional cattle grazing and dyke management are constantly being used to improve the breeding success of these wading birds. Redshank chicks can be spotted feeding in the damp grassy hollows left by winter flooding, gorging on the variety of insects.

STAR SPECIES

Norfolk hawker dragonfly

Frogbit

Water soldier

The blue-tailed damselfly is one of the most common

Frogbit

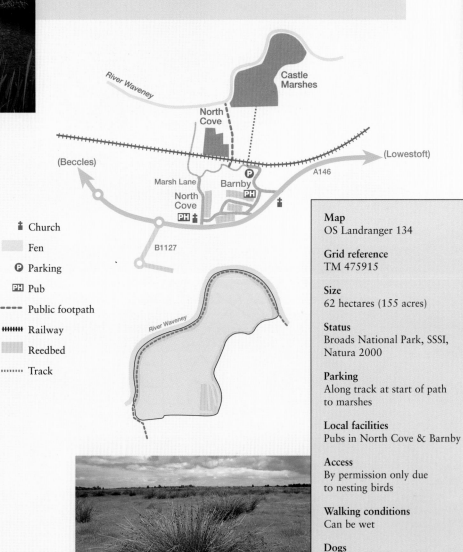

The areas of reed and taller vegetation between the river wall and the marshes are home to breeding birds including reed, sedge and grasshopper warbler.

As access to this reserve is restricted please contact Suffolk Wildlife Trust before visiting. The river wall is a public footpath and is therefore open at all times.

Other Trust reserves nearby: North Cove

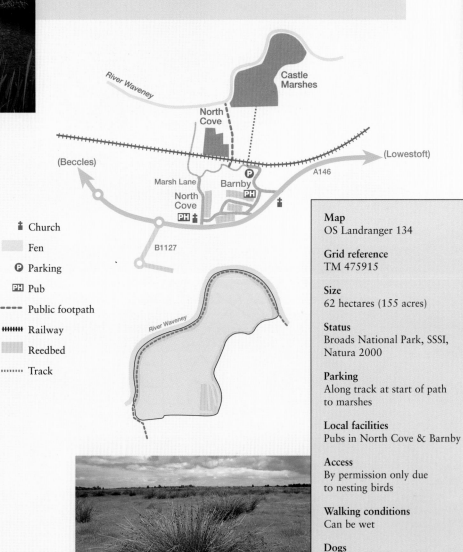

CASTLE MARSHES

Legend

- ⚑ Church
- Fen
- 🅿 Parking
- PH Pub
- ---- Public footpath
- ┼┼┼┼ Railway
- Reedbed
- ······· Track

Map
OS Landranger 134

Grid reference
TM 475915

Size
62 hectares (155 acres)

Status
Broads National Park, SSSI, Natura 2000

Parking
Along track at start of path to marshes

Local facilities
Pubs in North Cove & Barnby

Access
By permission only due to nesting birds

Walking conditions
Can be wet

Dogs
Sorry no dogs

Best time to visit
May–Sept

Round-headed club rush

COMBS WOOD

"A verdant cathedral. Woods as old as this are like ancient cities – full of well-established and complex communities."

Combs Wood is recorded in the Domesday Book as '*a wood for16 swine*' and it is likely that this site has always been woodland since primeval forest followed the Ice Age. As you walk around take a few moments to look at the large perimeter banks which are a typical feature of ancient woodlands.

Early-purple orchid carpet the woodland floor in sprin

One ride, known as Prospect Avenue, was cut in the 18th century when the wood was connected to Combs Hall by a now long forgotten formal garden. The wood's ancient origin and centuries of coppicing - a traditional way of harvesting timber - are responsible for the blankets of wildflowers. A sunny day in April or May elicits a riot of birdsong from chiffchaff, willow warbler, nightingale and blackcap. This is a good time to admire the plant life too as it is in full splendour with displays of early-purple orchid, ransom and bugle.

STAR SPECIES

Oxlip

Treecreeper

Greater butterfly orchid

The traditional art of charcoal burning benefits woodland wildlife

Specialities to look out for include moschatel, greater butterfly orchid, oxlip and wood anemone. Where nectar rich plants thrive so do many woodland butterfly including the orange tip and majestic peacock. To encourage this spectacular show Suffolk Wildlife Trust continue to manage the wood in the traditional way and charcoal burners, who harvest the coppice, can often be seen tending their smouldering pyre.

Other Trust reserves nearby: Bonny Wood

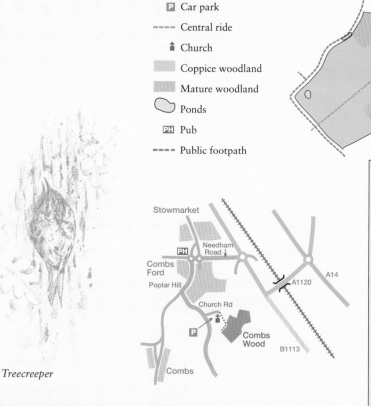

P	Car park
----	Central ride
⛪	Church
▓	Coppice woodland
▓	Mature woodland
◯	Ponds
PH	Pub
----	Public footpath

Treecreeper

Map
OS Landranger 155

Grid reference
TM 054568

Size
16.6 hectares (41.5 acres)

Status
SSSI

Parking
Near Combs Church

Local facilities
Combs Ford

Walking conditions
Boggy in winter and spring

Dogs
Sorry no dogs, sensitive site

Best time to visit
April–May

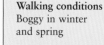

The 'eye' markings on peacock butterfly wings phase potential predators

CORNARD MERE

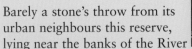

"Sometimes it feels like you're miles from civilisation. Although small, the Mere can throw up some surprises in terms of visiting wildlife."

Barely a stone's throw from its urban neighbours this reserve, lying near the banks of the River Stour, is special for its mix of open water, fen and wet scrub. Reed sweet-grass and common reed often dominate, providing nesting sites for reed bunting, sedge and reed warbler. In autumn swallow and sand martin stop off on their momentous journey back to Africa. Pied wagtail, fieldfare and redwing roost in the willow scrub in winter.

July and August are the best months to visit to appreciate the plants in their full glory. Parts of the reserve are mown every year to encourage flowers such as skullcap and greater bird's-foot trefoil and wintering birds like snipe. The piles of reed you may see have been deliberately left to provide homes for grass snake.

Dragonflies such as the ruddy darter and four-spotted chaser hover over the new areas of open water which are fringed with marginal aquatic plants such as bogbean and meadow rue. Large noctule bat can also be spotted hunting on summer evenings.

Cornard Mere is cared for by Suffolk Wildlife Trust and is jointly owned by the Trust and Cornard Parish Council.

STAR SPECIES
Snipe

Bogbean

Grass snake

Other Trust reserves nearby: Spouse's Vale

Noctule bat

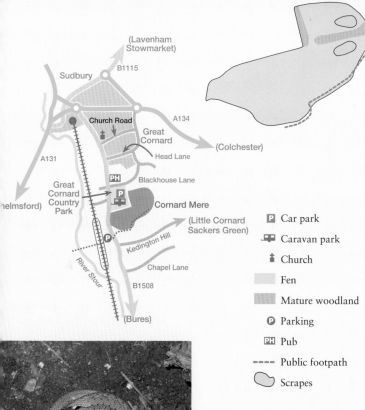

(Lavenham
Stowmarket)

B1115

Sudbury

Church Road

A134

Great
Cornard

Head Lane

(Colchester)

A131

Blackhouse Lane

PH

P

Great
Cornard
Country
Park

helmsford)

Cornard Mere

(Little Cornard
Sackers Green)

Kedington Hill

P

River Stour

Chapel Lane

B1508

(Bures)

P Car park

Caravan park

Church

Fen

Mature woodland

P Parking

PH Pub

---- Public footpath

Scrapes

*Grass snake can lay up to 40 eggs
in the warmth of old tree stumps
or compost heaps. They like damp
places and are good swimmers.*

Map
OS Landranger 155

Grid reference
TL 887388

Size
6 hectares (15 acres)

Status
SSSI

Parking
Great Cornard Country
Park or off B1508 near
Keddington Hill

Local facilities
Great Cornard

Walking conditions
Always damp;
can be very wet

Dogs
On leads only

Best time to visit
Feb, June–Aug

DARSHAM MARSHES

"A tranquil, lonely place made up of a mosaic of marsh and fen."

Carpets of rich pinks and yellows are likely to greet visitors, as the spectacular flowering plants burst into life during spring and early summer. Ragged-robin, yellow flag, marsh marigold and southern marsh orchid are all easy to spot.

A network of dykes and two ponds provide a rich habitat for a wealth of watery wildlife. In summer, long after the toad and frog multitudes have spawned, pause by the ponds to watch the acrobatic antics of dragonflies and damselflies. These nimble aeronauts, which include the scarce hairy dragonfly, are defending their territories. Look out too for grass snake soaking up the sun close to the footpath.

In winter hen harrier are on patrol and snipe scan for juicy worms along the edges of pools and ditches. Surrounding hedgerows provide berries for flocks of wintering fieldfare and redwing. In May the distinctive song of reed, sedge and grasshopper warbler can be heard among the fen vegetation. Barn owl and marsh harrier hunt over the marsh all year.

STAR SPECIES

Otter

Southern marsh orchid

Snipe

In Suffolk, barn owl are making a comeback after numbers plummeted in the 1950s due to habitat loss and pesticide poisoning

Otter, though seldom seen, leave their droppings in gateways and on bridges. Water vole also live here, although the characteristic 'plop' as they dive into the water means they have seen you first – they'll often reappear if you wait quietly!

The marshes were kindly donated to Suffolk Wildlife Trust by the Rodocanachi family in 1984. Through management with grazing cattle and sheep they have been restored to their former glory.

Other Trust reserves nearby: Dingle Marshes, Sizewell Belts

S. Aylward

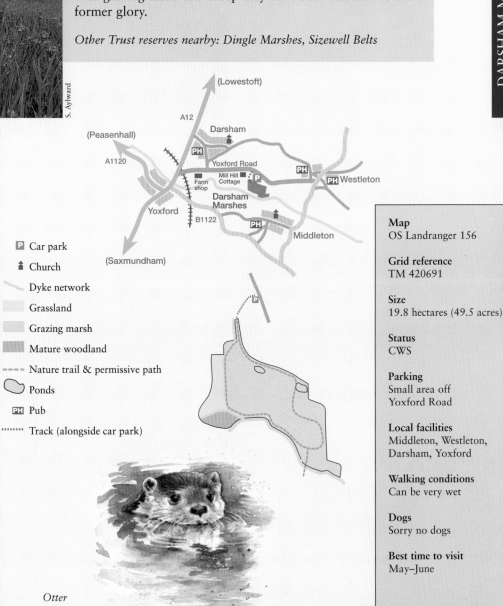

Legend:
- **P** Car park
- ⛪ Church
- Dyke network
- Grassland
- Grazing marsh
- Mature woodland
- - - - Nature trail & permissive path
- Ponds
- **PH** Pub
- ········ Track (alongside car park)

Map
OS Landranger 156

Grid reference
TM 420691

Size
19.8 hectares (49.5 acres)

Status
CWS

Parking
Small area off Yoxford Road

Local facilities
Middleton, Westleton, Darsham, Yoxford

Walking conditions
Can be very wet

Dogs
Sorry no dogs

Best time to visit
May–June

Otter

DINGLE MARSHES

"The attraction? Savouring the peace while standing in the middle of the largest freshwater reedbed in Britain with bittern booming and harrier hovering in the air above."

Dingle Marshes is one of the few places in Suffolk, accessible by road, where you can have a near wilderness experience. There's something exciting to see every day, but May is wonderful with bittern booming and marsh harrier displaying.

The reserve is a magnet for breeding and wintering wildfowl and wading birds including the elegant avocet, white-fronted goose, lapwing and redshank. The reedbed holds a significant proportion of the UK's marsh harrier and bittern – a shy bird of which there are only 13 booming males left in Britain.

The vulnerable otter and water vole also live here and the site is internationally important for starlet sea anemone – the rarest sea anemone in Britain. These live in the soft mud at the edges of the creeks, saltmarshes and brackish pools, are less than two centimetres long and feed on small shrimp-like creatures and snails.

This valuable reserve is looked after by a unique partnership involving Suffolk Wildlife Trust, RSPB and English Nature.

STAR SPECIES
Bittern
Marsh harrier
Avocet

Imagine the bittern's haunting call carrying for miles over marshland wilderness

By working together water levels are controlled, marshes grazed by cattle and reedbeds cut commercially for the benefit of wildlife. Dingle Marshes is jointly owned by Suffolk Wildlife Trust and RSPB.

Other Trust reserves nearby: Darsham Marshes

Starlet sea anemone

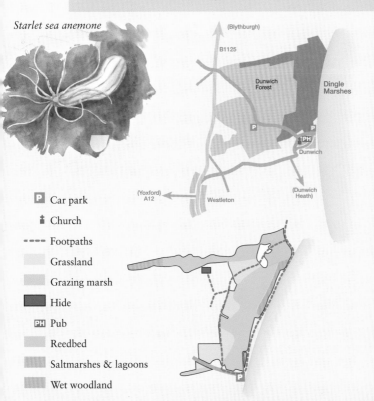

P   Car park

⚲   Church

----   Footpaths

    Grassland

    Grazing marsh

    Hide

PH   Pub

    Reedbed

    Saltmarshes & lagoons

    Wet woodland

Map
OS Landranger 156

Grid reference
TM 480720

Size
263 hectares (650 acres)

Status
SSSI, NNR, Natura 2000

Parking
Forest Enterprise car park
off Blythburgh Road
(for bird-hide access) &
Dunwich Beach car park

Local facilities
Dunwich

Walking conditions
Good all year

Dogs
On leads only

Best time to visit
All year

FOXBURROW FARM

"Hearing nightingale in Cragpit Wood and skylark above the set-aside fields is nothing short of magical!"

A visit to this small mixed farm during spring and early summer will be rewarded with spring flowers, birdsong and gambolling lambs. Little owl are sometimes seen in daylight perched on posts, and listen out for singing nightingale in the elder and bramble thickets at the farm's two woodlands – Asylum and Cragpit Woods. Blackcap, whitethroat and garden warbler can be seen in the woods and hedges, skylark nest in the meadows and spotted flycatcher and pied wagtail flit around the farm buildings.

The arable land is managed commercially through a tenant farmer, while the farm's meadows are grazed by Suffolk Wildlife Trust's Sandlings sheep flock. Hedges, which have been coppiced and replanted, provide a great source of winter food and act as wildlife corridors allowing insects, birds and mammals to travel from place to place without having to cross open farmland. Foxburrow is a good example of how modern agriculture and wildlife can thrive side by side.

STAR SPECIES
Little owl
Nightingale
Skylark

Farm buildings with Sandlings sheep flock

Water boatman

Although nocturnal, little owl can sometimes be seen perched on a post during daylight.

A dipping platform at one of six ponds allows exploration of watery wildlife

Six ponds team with water boatmen, pond skater, diving beetle, water scorpion, toad, frog and newt. From late May onwards dragonfly including the broad-bodied chaser and ruddy darter and damselfly such as the common blue and large red, can be seen hovering over ponds or laying eggs in the water.

A wander along the farm trails gives visitors a chance to see some of the work done by the Trust and our tenant farmers to improve the site's wildlife interest.

Other Trust reserves nearby: Bromeswell Green, Hutchison's Meadow

Common frog

Field vole

A well-equipped classroom caters for both children and adults

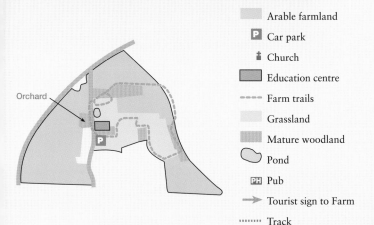

Orchard

- Arable farmland
- **P** Car park
- ⛪ Church
- Education centre
- - - - Farm trails
- Grassland
- Mature woodland
- Pond
- **PH** Pub
- → Tourist sign to Farm
- .... Track

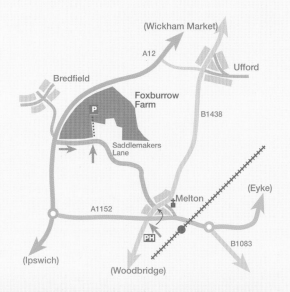

(Wickham Market)

A12

Ufford

Bredfield

Foxburrow
Farm

B1438

Saddlemakers
Lane

(Eyke)

Melton

A1152

PH

(Ipswich)

B1083

(Woodbridge)

Map
OS Landranger 156

Grid reference
TM 275515

Size
53 hectares (132.5 acres)

Status
SWT owned farm
Education and visitor centre

Parking
On site

Local facilities
Melton, Woodbridge

Walking conditions
Good, can be muddy
in winter

Dogs
Sorry no dogs

Wheelchair/pushchair access

Best time to visit
April–June

FOXBURROW WOOD

"A haven of calm in a hectic sea of housing and traffic."

Need a break from the hustle and bustle of town? This inviting wood on the Northern outskirts of Lowestoft is guaranteed to refresh the most jaded of visitors. In spring contrasting colours of fresh flowering bluebells, greater stitchwort and wood anemone combine to make a fine show. Other flowers typical of ancient woodland like twayblade, early-purple orchid and primrose, add to the scene at this unique urban oasis.

Mature sweet chestnut, oak, birch, sycamore, alder and ash trees are complemented by a series of ponds, ditches and streams where yellow marsh marigold, mauve water mint and common newt and frog thrive. Birds such as nuthatch, wood-pecker and treecreeper, joined by summer visiting blackcap, chiffchaff and willow warbler, create a delightful song.

Foxburrow Wood is cared for by Suffolk Wildlife Trust on behalf of Waveney District Council.

STAR SPECIES
Wood anemone

Bluebell

Other Trust reserves nearby: Camps Heath, Carlton Marshes, Castle Marshes, Oulton Marshes

Ash leaves

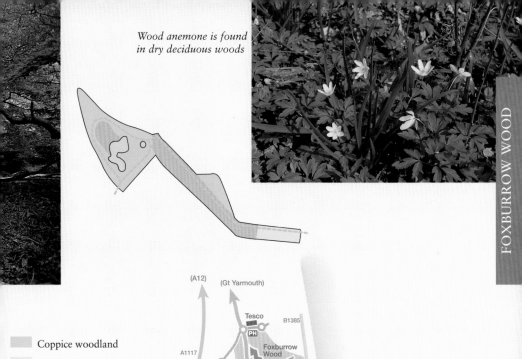

Wood anemone is found in dry deciduous woods

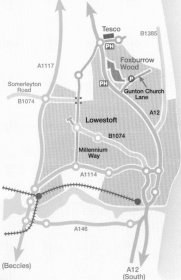

Legend:
- Coppice woodland
- Grassland
- Mature woodland
- - - - Nature trail
- **P** Parking
- Ponds
- PH Pub
- :: Traffic lights

(A12)
(Gt Yarmouth)

Tesco
B1385
Foxburrow Wood
A1117
Somerleyton Road
B1074
Gunton Church Lane
A12
Lowestoft
B1074
Millennium Way
A1114
A146
(Beccles)
A12 (South)

Map
OS Landranger 134

Grid reference
TL 537955

Size
4 hectares (10 acres)

Status
CWS, LNR

Parking
Gunton Church Lane

Local facilities
Foxburrow Beefeater
Travel Inn nearby on A12

Walking conditions
Muddy when wet

Dogs
On leads only

Best time to visit
April, May

Treecreeper climb up trees searching for insects in the bark

GROTON WOOD

"Enchanting walks take you down sheltered rides, where brimstone butterflies feed on sunny spring days and woodcock display at dusk."

This ancient woodland is noted for its small-leaved lime coppice – an indication that the northern part has existed since prehistoric times. The southern section dates back to the 17th century being mainly oak, hazel, ash and wild cherry – a favourite food of the resident but shy hawfinch best seen in the early morning. The wood's 22 mostly seasonal ponds are good places to spot frog, toad and newt including the protected great-crested newt.

Flowers like violet helleborine, woodruff, herb-paris, bluebell, pignut and early-purple orchid look a treat in spring and the 15 species of butterfly include brimstone, speckled wood and purple hairstreak whose caterpillars feed on oak. The endearing dormouse makes its home in the hazel coppice.

Summer songsters include nightingale, while other birds like treecreeper, all three woodpecker species, woodcock and nuthatch are resident here. Like many of Suffolk Wildlife Trust's woodland reserves much of this site is managed by coppicing, which involves cutting sections of woodland on a rotational basis to prolong life, increase diversity and encourage re-growth.

STAR SPECIES

Small-leaved lime

Hawfinch

Violet helleborine

Mating brimstone butterfly

Common toad are among the many amphibians drawn to the wood's ponds

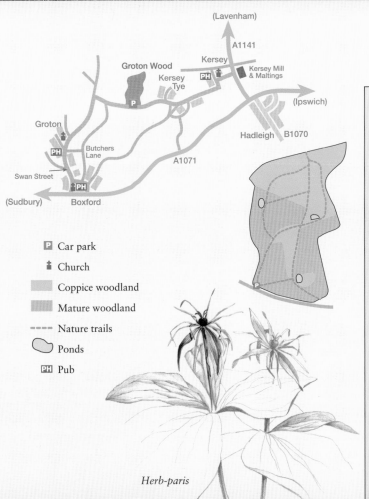

(Lavenham)

A1141

Kersey

Groton Wood

Kersey Mill
& Maltings

Kersey
Tye

PH

P

(Ipswich)

Groton

Hadleigh   B1070

PH

Butchers
Lane

Swan Street

A1071

PH

(Sudbury)   Boxford

P   Car park

✝   Church

        Coppice woodland

        Mature woodland

- - - -   Nature trails

        Ponds

PH   Pub

Herb-paris

Map
OS Landranger 155

Grid reference
TL 977428

Size
21 hectares (52.5 acres)

Status
SSSI

Parking
At entrance to reserve

Local facilities
Groton, Kersey

Walking conditions
Can be muddy

Dogs
On lead only

Best time to visit
May, June

GROVE FARM

"The meadows on this mixed farm are like a piece of forgotten Suffolk with their skylark and wildflowers."

There's always something special to see here at Grove Farm where conservation and commercial farming can be seen working side by side. Left to the Trust by Mrs Cooper in 1995 this reserve is managed under a Farm Business Tenancy and a good circular walk takes in all the habitats on the farm.

In spring skylark can be seen hovering above the set aside fields and snipe spend the winter in the meadows. Plants like southern marsh orchid, marsh marigold, marsh valerian and ragged-robin bloom in the wet meadows bordering the River Black Bourn, in early summer. On the higher, drier land flowers like self heal, ox-eye daisy and common cat's-ear can be found.

Dense mixed hedges consist of hawthorn, hazel, dog rose, oak and willow. Secretive otter have been spotted on the grazing marshes and intersecting dykes.

During harvest in July/August please contact Suffolk Wildlife Trust before visiting.

Other Trust reserves nearby: Bradfield Woods

STAR SPECIES

Skylark

Hare

Southern marsh orchid

Skylarks' inconspicuous nests blend in with the surroundings

The hare's spring courtship ritual involves spectacular boxing, leaping and chasing

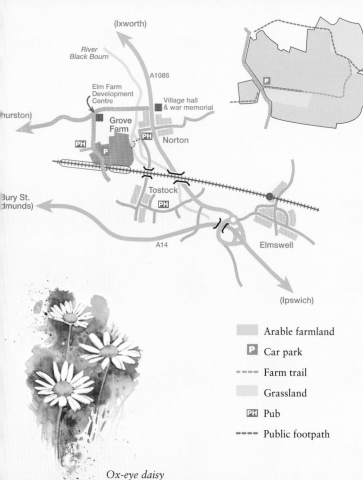

(Ixworth)

River
Black Bourn

A1088

Elm Farm
Development
Centre

Village hall
& war memorial

(hurston)

Grove
Farm

Norton

PH

PH

P

(Bury St.
Edmunds)

Tostock

PH

A14

Elmswell

(Ipswich)

P

Ox-eye daisy

Arable farmland
P Car park
---- Farm trail
Grassland
PH Pub
---- Public footpath

Map
OS Landranger 155

Grid reference
TL 943652

Size
62.3 hectares (155.75 acres)

Status
CWS

Parking
Off road

Local facilities
Norton

Walking conditions
Can be muddy

Dogs
On lead only

Best time to visit
May, June

THE HAVEN, THORPENESS

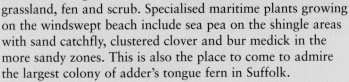

*"An amazing diversity
of plants survive
thousands of trampling
feet, grazing rabbits and
salt laden winds!
Surely a great testimony
to nature's power of
survival against all
the odds."*

The Haven is an exposed
mosaic of shingle, dune
grassland, fen and scrub. Specialised maritime plants growing
on the windswept beach include sea pea on the shingle areas
with sand catchfly, clustered clover and bur medick in the
more sandy zones. This is also the place to come to admire
the largest colony of adder's tongue fern in Suffolk.

One of our largest insects, the fabulous great green bush
cricket, has its home here. Unlike grasshopper these striking
creatures, which are around five centimetres long, are likely
to crawl rather than hop and are more active in the evening,
singing until well into the night.

The scrub and reedbed on the west side of the road, are good
for marsh harrier and migrant birds taking a break before
and after their long African journey.

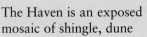

The Haven is cared for by Suffolk
Wildlife Trust on behalf of the RSPB
who also own North Warren nature
reserve adjacent to this site.

Other Trust reserves nearby:
Darsham Marshes, Hazelwood Marshes

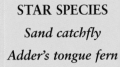

STAR SPECIES
Sand catchfly
Adder's tongue fern

Great green bush cricket

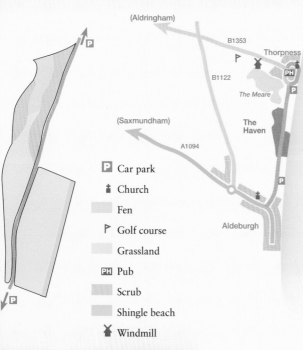

(Aldringham)

B1353

Thorpness

B1122

The Meare

(Saxmundham)

A1094

The Haven

PH

Aldeburgh

P Car park

♗ Church

Fen

⚐ Golf course

Grassland

PH Pub

Scrub

Shingle beach

⚑ Windmill

Map
OS Landranger 156

Grid reference
TM 470585

Size
16 hectares (40 acres)

Status
CWS, SSSI

Parking
Aldeburgh &
Thorpeness car parks

Local facilities
Aldeburgh, Thorpeness

Walking conditions
Dry all year

Dogs
Kept under control

Best time to visit
March–July, Sept, Oct

*Shingle flowers like sea pea
are sensitive to disturbance*

HAZELWOOD MARSHES

"Surrounded by a haunting, evocative landscape – the place that time forgot"

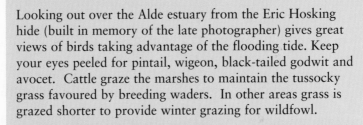

There are fabulous views from the Hazelwood hide on to Ham Creek

Hazelwood Marshes are one of the last undrained grazing marshes on the Suffolk coast and among the most important for breeding wading birds including redshank, snipe and lapwing and wintering wildfowl such as white-fronted geese. Marsh harrier, barn owl and avocet also nest here.

Looking out over the Alde estuary from the Eric Hosking hide (built in memory of the late photographer) gives great views of birds taking advantage of the flooding tide. Keep your eyes peeled for pintail, wigeon, black-tailed godwit and avocet. Cattle graze the marshes to maintain the tussocky grass favoured by breeding waders. In other areas grass is grazed shorter to provide winter grazing for wildfowl.

A network of fresh and brackish water dykes dissects the grazing marsh. These act like wet fences to control the cattle and provide a valuable wildlife habitat. In some stretches of fresh water the flowerless stems of stonewort are just visible below the surface. This is not a true plant, but an algae which flourishes in clean, still water. In the brackish areas, look out for soft hornwort and horned pondweed. Reed fringes are home to breeding birds such as sedge and reed warbler and bearded tit, as well as dragonflies like the black-tailed skimmer and scarce chaser.

*Other Trust reserves nearby:
The Haven Thorpeness, Sizewell Belts*

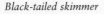

Black-tailed skimmer

STAR SPECIES
Redshank
Snipe
Black-tailed godwit

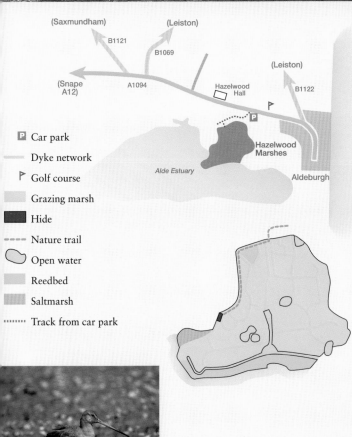

Map
OS Landranger 156

Grid reference
TM 435575

Size
62.4 hectares (156 acres)

Status
SSSI, Natura 2000

Parking
Off Aldeburgh Rd,
0.5km from reserve

Local facilities
Snape, Aldeburgh

Walking conditions
Wet in winter

Dogs
No dogs please

Best time to visit
Nov–Feb

Key:
- P Car park
- Dyke network
- Golf course
- Grazing marsh
- Hide
- Nature trail
- Open water
- Reedbed
- Saltmarsh
- Track from car park

Map labels: (Saxmundham), (Leiston), B1121, B1069, (Leiston), (Snape A12), A1094, Hazelwood Hall, B1122, Hazelwood Marshes, Alde Estuary, Aldeburgh

Black-tailed godwit

HEN REEDBED

"A rich mosaic of wonderful wetland habitat and a real treat for anyone interested in birds."

Hen Reedbed is a blend of reedbeds, fens, dykes and pools created in 1999 to provide new breeding habitat for bittern and other wildlife.

In summer look out for marsh harrier, heron, bearded tit and even hobby hunting over the reeds and dykes. Reed and sedge warblers sing to their hearts' content alongside clouds of iridescent damselfly and nimble dragonfly such as the four-spot chaser and hairy dragonfly. Far more secretive are the otter and water vole which also live here.

For the best views of the largest mere follow the way-marked trail through the reedbed to the viewing platform at Wolsey Creek Marshes. Here the pools are good places to spot wildfowl such as gadwall, tufted duck and teal. At low tide scan the mudflats behind you for feeding waders – redshank, avocet and sandpiper are all regulars.

A lay-by on the A1095 gives access to Norman Gwatkin Marshes, the oldest part of the reserve. The hide at the end of the path overlooks grazing marsh, which is part of Henham Estate. In summer look along the reed-fringed dykes for reed warbler, marsh harrier and heron – the heronry is one of the largest in Suffolk. Rich pickings around the dykes encourage otter, water vole and the graceful grass snake.

STAR SPECIES

Marsh harrier

Bearded tit

Water vole

Marsh harrier are usually seen flying low over the reedbed

The damp woodland is dominated by sallow, osier and alder and is good for fungi, fern and wetland plants like skull-cap and lesser water-parsnip.

Other Trust reserves nearby: Reydon Wood, Wenhaston Commons

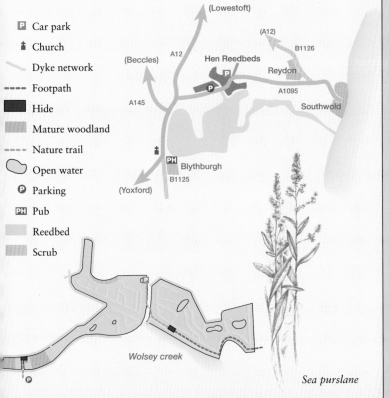

P Car park

⚑ Church

Dyke network

---- Footpath

■ Hide

▨ Mature woodland

---- Nature trail

⬭ Open water

P Parking

PH Pub

▨ Reedbed

▨ Scrub

(Lowestoft)

(A12)

B1126

A12

Hen Reedbeds

Reydon

(Beccles)

A1095

A145

Southwold

⚑

PH Blythburgh

B1125

(Yoxford)

Wolsey creek

Sea purslane

Map
OS Landranger 156

Grid reference
TM 470770

Size
44.2 hectares (110.5 acres)

Status
SSSI, NNR, RAMSAR, Natura 2000

Parking
At lay-by on A1095 and the main car park at reserve sign

Local facilities
Reydon, Southwold

Walking conditions
Good. Wet in wood – path recommended

Dogs
On leads only – sorry no dogs in hide

Best time to visit
April, May

HOPTON FEN

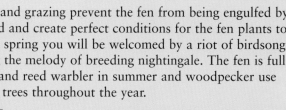

HOPTON FEN

"There is a wonderful sense of seclusion. The changing hues from winter silver to the dark gold of an autumn sunset, add beautiful seasonal subtleties."

This is a gem of a site for the fen enthusiast. The waterlogged peat allows unique plants and animals to flourish. Bristling stands of saw sedge, reed and rushes dominate with scatterings of rare plants such as black bog rush, southern, marsh fragrant and early marsh orchid, adder's tongue fern, twayblade and bogbean. Hemp agrimony and the azure blue Devil's-bit scabious flower later in the season.

Mowing and grazing prevent the fen from being engulfed by woodland and create perfect conditions for the fen plants to thrive. In spring you will be welcomed by a riot of birdsong including the melody of breeding nightingale. The fen is full of sedge and reed warbler in summer and woodpecker use the older trees throughout the year.

Hopton Fen is leased by Suffolk Wildlife Trust from Hopton Combined Charities.

Other Trust reserves nearby: Market Weston Fen, Redgrave & Lopham Fen, Thelnetham Fen

Devil's-bit scabious

M. J. Thomas

STAR SPECIES

Marsh fragrant orchid

Reed warbler

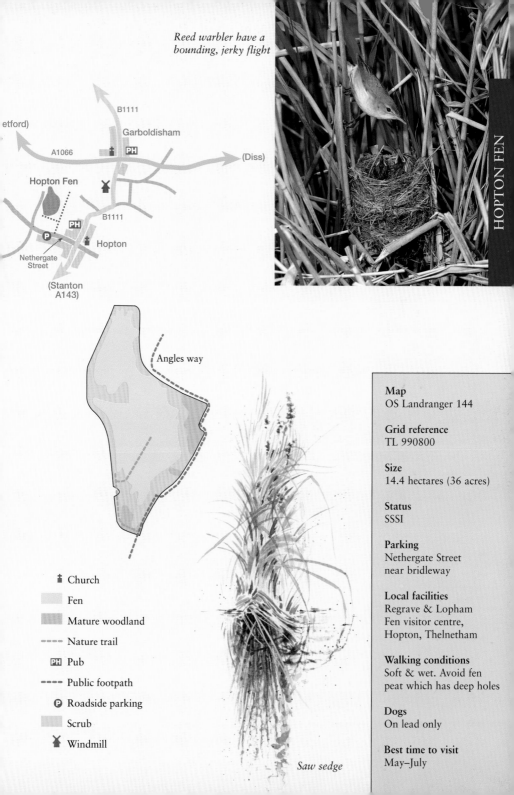

Reed warbler have a bounding, jerky flight

HOPTON FEN

Map
OS Landranger 144

Grid reference
TL 990800

Size
14.4 hectares (36 acres)

Status
SSSI

Parking
Nethergate Street
near bridleway

Local facilities
Regrave & Lopham
Fen visitor centre,
Hopton, Thelnetham

Walking conditions
Soft & wet. Avoid fen
peat which has deep holes

Dogs
On lead only

Best time to visit
May–July

Angles way

ⓣ Church

    Fen

    Mature woodland

----- Nature trail

PH Pub

---- Public footpath

Ⓟ Roadside parking

    Scrub

✗ Windmill

Saw sedge

HURST FEN & HOWLETT HILLS

"There's something for everyone here from woodland and ponds to grassland and fen."

The beauty of this reserve, located about 1km down Eldon Lane, lies in its many different habitats all of which are within a relatively small area. Situated on the edge of Breckland it displays a typical range of sand, grassland, fen, scrub and secondary woodland which host plants such as meadow saxifrage, yellow loosestrife, small scabious, greater water-parsnip and saw sedge.

Two uncommon sedges – long-stalked yellow sedge and carnation sedge – have recently made a comeback following work to clear scrub and control water levels. Woodcock, kingfisher, grass snake, smooth newt, frog, ruddy darter and broad-bodied chaser dragonfly can also be seen. Look out for the white admiral butterfly with its unmistakeable gliding flight.

Hurst Fen & Howlett Hills is cared for by Suffolk Wildlife Trust on behalf of Mildenhall Parish Council.

Other Trust reserves nearby: Brandon Artemisia, Norah Hanbury-Kelk Meadows, Rex Graham, Wangford Warren

The smooth newt is the most widespread in Britain and is often found in garden ponds

STAR SPECIES

Greater water-parsnip

White admiral butterfly

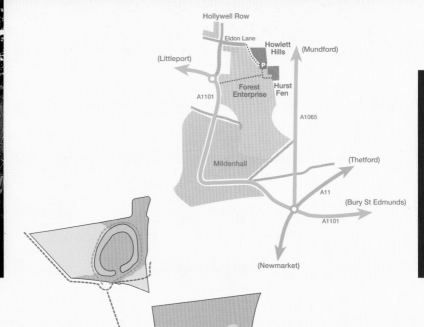

Hollywell Row

Eldon Lane

Howlett Hills

(Mundford)

(Littleport)

Forest Enterprise

Hurst Fen

A1101

A1065

Mildenhall

(Thetford)

A11

(Bury St Edmunds)

A1101

(Newmarket)

P Car park

Fen

- - - - Footpath

Grassland

- - - - Nature trail

Woodland

Streams, ditches

White admiral butterfly

Greater water-parsnip

Map
OS Landranger 143

Grid reference
TL 722769

Size
8.4 hectares (21 acres)

Status
CWS

Parking
Approx 1km down
Eldon Lane at
Howlett Hills

Walking conditions
Uneven, can be
wet & boggy

Dogs
On leads only

Best time to visit
All year

HUTCHISON'S MEADOW

"An uplifting oasis of rough grassland in a fast developing suburbia."

Hutchison's Meadow is an inspiring example of flower-rich grassland. Since 1939, virtually all of Suffolk's flower-rich meadows have been destroyed through development or changes in agricultural practice. Only fragments like this remain.

The wetter areas feature colourful displays of ragged-robin, common fleabane, square-stalked St John's-wort and there is a superb colony of southern marsh orchid. Yellow flowered tormentil can be found in the drier areas.

Look out for green woodpecker in the open meadow searching the grass for ants and grubs. You are welcome to walk around the margins of the meadow, but please avoid trampling the flowers. As the variety of flowers are maintained by grazing with sheep throughout the year, we regret that dogs are not allowed on the meadow at any time.

The meadow was kindly donated to Suffolk Wildlife Trust by Sir Peter and Lady Hutchison.

Other Trust reserves nearby: Bromeswell Green, Foxburrow Farm

Common fleabane

Southern marsh orchid can vary in colour from pale pink through to deep purple

STAR SPECIES

Southern marsh orchid

Ragged-robin

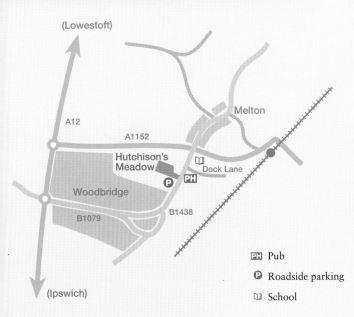

(Lowestoft)

A12

A1152

Melton

Hutchison's
Meadow

Dock Lane

Woodbridge

P PH

B1438

B1079

(Ipswich)

PH Pub

P Roadside parking

School

Map
OS Landranger 156

Grid reference
TM 279501

Size
0.5 hectares (1.25 acres)

Status
CWS

Parking
Roadside

Local facilities
Local pub opposite

Walking conditions
Can be wet in winter

Dogs
No dogs due to
grazing sheep

Best time to visit
May, June

*With its laughing call
you're likely to hear a
green woodpecker before
you see one!*

LACKFORD LAKES

"The reserve can provide a magical 'close encounter' with nature, be it the turquoise flash of a kingfisher, the splendour of a fishing osprey or the sheer charm of a brood of new ducklings."

Lackford Lakes lie beside the River Lark and have been created from former gravel pits. The potential list of birds here seems never ending, with rarities like hoopoe occurring alongside more common species such as shelduck.

A superb site for wildfowl in both winter and summer, Lackford attracts tufted duck, pochard, gadwall, shoveler and goosander. There is a large winter gull roost and one or two pairs of redshank nest here – unusual so far from the coast.

Passing birds of prey include the majestic osprey, whilst hobby and goshawk can also be spotted – the former in hot pursuit of sand martin and the many dragonflies. This is one of the best places in Suffolk for kingfisher, and cormorant are often seen fishing at the sailing lake or roosting in the tall trees by the river. Almost any migrant bird can turn up – black tern are regulars but species like Caspian tern, spoonbill and the more uncommon waders are also seen.

STAR SPECIES

Pochard

Kingfisher

Migrant birds

Common storks-bill grows up to 30cm (1ft) high

The kingfisher's vantage point above the water, enables it to plunge after unsuspecting prey

Male tufted duck can be identified by their long head crest

Otter

LACKFORD LAKES

This reclaimed site has been quickly colonised by plants. Gipsywort, figwort, common fleabane and purple loosestrife occur by the water's edge and common centaury and common stork's-bill appear in the drier areas. Encroaching sallows need to be kept in check so that the open water, which hosts clouds of blue damselfies, is not lost. The otter has become a frequent visitor here.

Suffolk Wildlife Trust's original 11 hectare reserve at Lackford was donated by Bernard Tickner in 1976. In 2000 RMC donated a further 90 hectares of land to form the Lackford Lakes reserve. With funding from RMC's Environment Fund and a Trust appeal, a range of improvements are being made to the reserve for wildlife and people. As part of this the Trust will open a visitor and education centre in 2002.

Other Trust reserves nearby:
Norah Hanbury-Kelk Meadows, Rex Graham

C. Jakes

The broad-bodied chaser dragonfly is highly territorial and can possessively hog a boundary marker, like a stone or reed, for days on end

Osprey feet are specially adapted to catch and grip slippery fish and eels

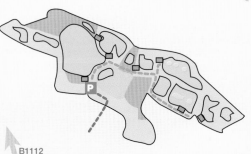

LACKFORD LAKES

---- Access track

P Car park

🛉 Church

⚐ Golf course

■ Grassland

■ Heath

■ Hides

◗ Lakes

▥ Mature woodland

---- Nature trail

PH Pub

➔ Tourist sign

B1112

(Mildenhall)

Icklingham
PH

River Lark   A1101

West Stow
Country Park   Lackford
Lakes   West Stow

P

Lackford   ⚐
PH

Flempton

(Bury St. Edmunds)

Map
OS Landranger 155

Grid reference
TL 803708

Size
101 hectares (253 acres)

Status
SSSI
Visitor centre opens 2002

Parking
Reserve entrance

Local facilities
West Stow Country Park,
Flempton, Icklingham

Walking conditions
Good

Dogs
Sorry no dogs

Wheelchair/pushchair
Access to one hide

Best time to visit
All year

LADYGATE WOOD

"Perched on a hilltop on the edge of Haverhill this is a woodland oasis with a surprising range of trees for such a small site."

A wonderful variety of trees, including less common ones like wayfaring tree are found in this small ancient woodland. Ash, hazel, field maple, hawthorn and oak are all here as is woodland hawthorn.

Plants such as oxlip, wood avens, wood anemone and sanicle swell the ranks of the pretty spring flowers that make this site so appealing. Woodcock are sometimes seen and woodland birds such as great spotted woodpecker and nuthatch have plenty of nest sites to choose from.

To conserve the woodland's wildlife a programme of coppicing which involves cutting small areas of woodland on a rotational basis to encourage re-growth, is carried out.

Ladygate Wood is cared for by Suffolk Wildlife Trust on behalf of a private owner.

STAR SPECIES
Oxlip
Wood anemone
Nuthatch

Nuthatch   *Woodcock*

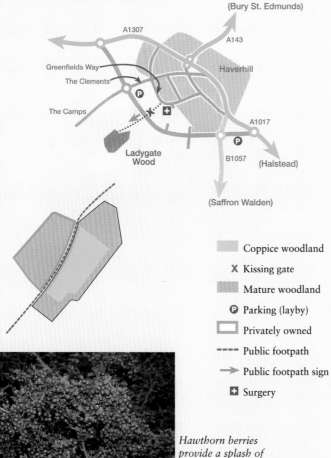

(Bury St. Edmunds)

A1307

A143

Greenfields Way
The Clements

Haverhill

The Camps

P

Ladygate
Wood

A1017

B1057

(Halstead)

(Saffron Walden)

Coppice woodland

X Kissing gate

Mature woodland

P Parking (layby)

Privately owned

---- Public footpath

→ Public footpath sign

✚ Surgery

*Hawthorn berries
provide a splash of
autumn colour*

Map
OS Landranger 154

Grid reference
TL 654442

Size
5.6 hectares (14 acres)

Status
CWS

Parking
Lay-by on Haverhill
by-pass

Local facilities
Haverhill

Walking conditions
Difficult when wet

Dogs
On leads only

Best time to visit
April, May

LAKENHEATH POORS FEN

"A remote area of original fen where the peace, birdsong and general absence of human activity creates a fine atmosphere."

This fen meadow is rich in wildflowers with an unusual mix of Breckland and fen plants including meadow rue, bugle, sneezewort and twayblade. Playful hare abound and the lovely song of birds like blackcap and nightingale can be heard in spring.

Insect life is abundant with many common species of butterfly such as wall and meadow brown, ringlet and gate keeper. Dragonfly hover above dykes containing lesser water-plantain and brookweed. This reserve is noted for its creeping willow while other trees include purging buckthorn, birch and crab apple.

This site is leased by Suffolk Wildlife Trust from Lakenheath Consolidated Charities.

Other Trust reserves nearby:
Brandon Artemisia, Pashford Poors Fen,
Wangford Warren

STAR SPECIES
Creeping willow
Sneezewort

Creeping willow

The blackcap is usually shy but may visit bird tables in winter

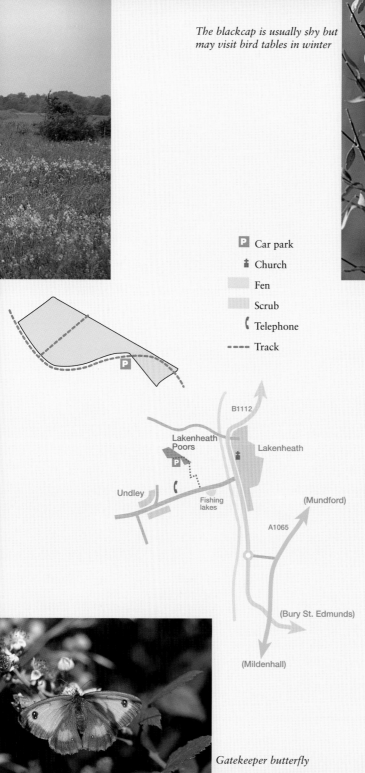

P	Car park
⛪	Church
▨	Fen
▨	Scrub
(	Telephone
----	Track

B1112

Lakenheath Poors

P

Lakenheath

Undley

Fishing lakes

(Mundford)

A1065

(Bury St. Edmunds)

(Mildenhall)

Gatekeeper butterfly

Map
OS Landranger 143

Grid reference
TL 705827

Size
4.7 hectares (11.75 acres)

Status
SSSI

Parking
Limited space at end of track

Local facilities
Lakenheath

Walking conditions
Can be marshy & muddy

Dogs
On leads only

Best time to visit
April–July

LANDGUARD

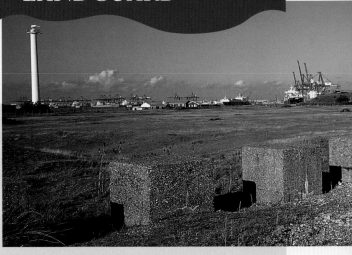

"Never a dull moment here! An exciting mix of sea and beach with the industrial backdrop of Britain's largest container port, Felixstowe Docks, and the austere military fort."

A must for anyone who wants to witness the spectacle of bird migration, explore the remarkable plant life or experience a wild, windswept peninsula with 500 years of military history.

Landguard is an exposed sand and shingle peninsula at the mouth of the River Orwell. Despite dramatic winter storms and scorching summer sun, rare shingle flowers, shore birds and a variety of migrants manage to thrive.

In April the short, rabbit cropped grass is studded with blue early forget-me-not, white clover, pink geranium and yellow medick. The open shingle turns almost white by late May as bushy sea kale flourishes. Then it's the turn of yellow-horned poppy followed by sheep's sorrel with its rusty orange hues. In spring and summer fenced off areas protect nesting ringed plover and little tern along with delicate plants such as the rare stinking goosefoot whose flowers resemble tiny broccoli florets!

In autumn numbers of migrating birds can be breathtaking and the nearby bird observatory has recorded 14 species new to Suffolk since 1982. Important breeding birds include little tern, ringed plover, oystercatcher and sometimes wheatear and black redstart.

STAR SPECIES

Stinking goosefoot

Little tern

Migrant birds

Little tern

As one of Suffolk Wildlife Trust's education centres, Landguard caters for local school children and other groups all year round.

Landguard is cared for by Suffolk Wildlife Trust on behalf of Suffolk County Council, Suffolk Coastal District Council and Harwich Haven Authority.

Other Trust reserves nearby: Trimley Marshes

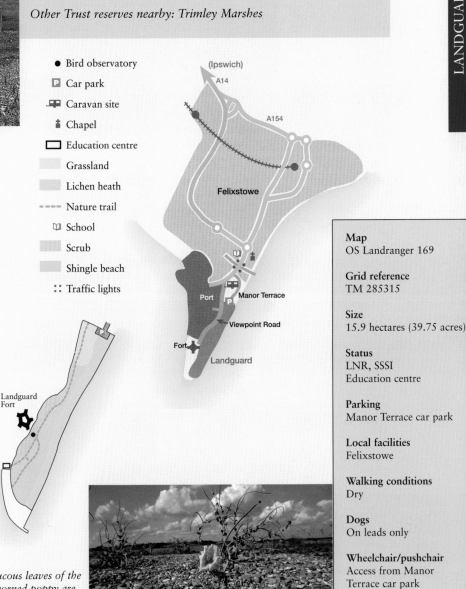

- ● Bird observatory
- **P** Car park
- Caravan site
- Chapel
- ☐ Education centre
-   Grassland
-   Lichen heath
- - - - Nature trail
- School
-   Scrub
-   Shingle beach
- ∷ Traffic lights

(Ipswich)
A14
A154
Felixstowe
Port
Manor Terrace
P
Viewpoint Road
Fort
Landguard

Landguard
Fort

Map
OS Landranger 169

Grid reference
TM 285315

Size
15.9 hectares (39.75 acres)

Status
LNR, SSSI
Education centre

Parking
Manor Terrace car park

Local facilities
Felixstowe

Walking conditions
Dry

Dogs
On leads only

Wheelchair/pushchair
Access from Manor
Terrace car park

Best time to visit
All year

The glaucous leaves of the yellow-horned poppy are tough enough to withstand harsh maritime conditions

LEVINGTON LAGOON

"Simply one of the best places for estuarine birds on the Orwell."

This brackish lagoon by the River Orwell was formed as a result of a breach in the sea wall during the notorious 1953 floods, which affected much of the east coast of England. This sensitive site is a magnet for breeding, wintering and passage estuarine birds of which there are exceptional numbers and variety.

For this reason Levington Lagoon makes a fantastic bird-watching site throughout the year. Seasonal specialities include greenshank, spotted redshank, dunlin, short-eared owl and flocks of pipit. You may also be lucky enough to spot kingfisher which seem to be something of a 'regular' here!

Saltmarsh plants include lilac drifts of sea lavender (which unlike its inland cousin has no scent) and sea purslane. Suffolk Wildlife Trust looks after this site by controlling water levels via a system of sluices to encourage wading birds.

Levington Lagoon is cared for by Suffolk Wildlife Trust on behalf of Suffolk Yacht Harbour Ltd.

STAR SPECIES

Sea lavender

Grey plover

Dunlin

*Other Trust reserves nearby:
Nacton Meadow, Trimley Marshes*

Grey plover

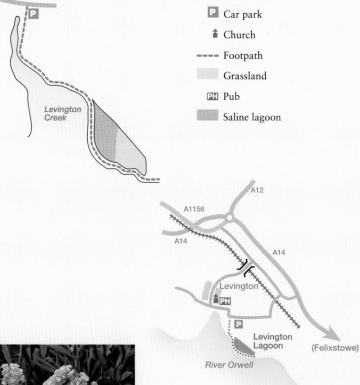

Car park 🅿

Church ⛪

Footpath - - - -

Grassland

Pub PH

Saline lagoon

Levington Creek

A12

A1156

A14

A14

Levington

PH

Levington Lagoon

(Felixstowe)

River Orwell

Map
OS Landranger 169

Grid reference
TM 239385

Size
0.3 hectares (0.75 acres)

Status
SSSI, Natura 2000

Parking
Off road at head of
Levington Creek by
footpath

Local facilities
Local pub nearby

Walking conditions
Can be wet & muddy

Dogs
Sorry no dogs,
sensitive site

Best time to visit
All year

*Stunning purple sea lavender
transforms the saltmarsh in summer*

"This fen seems to boast just about every botanical rarity possible for its small size – a classic example of just how rich a valley fen can be."

With over 250 flowering plants, 20 species of butterfly including white admiral and grayling, and 200 types of moth such as the oak eggar and dotted fan-foot Market Weston Fen is a wildlife paradise. It comes as no surprise to learn that it is one of the finest fragments of valley fen in East Anglia and is nationally and internationally important for wildlife.

A public footpath passes through the fen, or you can take the circular waymarked trail to explore other areas of the reserve. This takes you up onto higher ground and into a patchwork of scrub, heath and ponds before leading you back to the open fen, which is dominated by sedge beds.

Most of the sedge fen, used commercially to cap thatched roofs, is cut every 3-5 years. Fen meadow areas are cut annually. This regular harvesting allows a superb display of flowering fen plants to thrive particularly marsh lousewort, purple loosestrife, grass-of-Parnassus, marsh helleborine and insectivorous sundew.

STAR SPECIES

Grass-of-Parnassus

Grasshopper warbler

Common lizard

Purple loosestrife grows by the pond

Birds like snipe, sedge, reed and grasshopper warbler breed in the open fen and nightingale nest in the scrub. Keep a look out for kingfisher darting along the stream and the secretive common lizard basking in the sun.

Other Trust reserves nearby: Hopton Fen, Thelnetham Fen

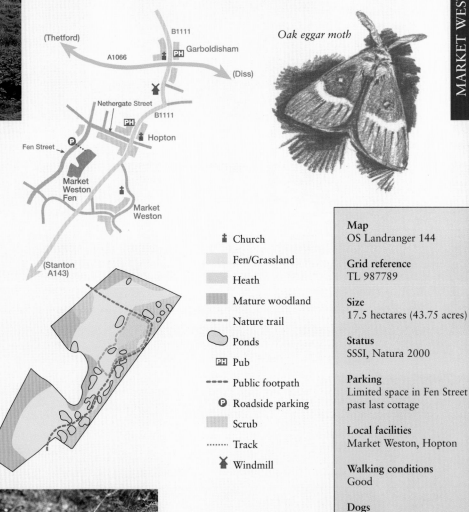

Oak eggar moth

Church
Fen/Grassland
Heath
Mature woodland
Nature trail
Ponds
Pub
Public footpath
Roadside parking
Scrub
Track
Windmill

Map
OS Landranger 144

Grid reference
TL 987789

Size
17.5 hectares (43.75 acres)

Status
SSSI, Natura 2000

Parking
Limited space in Fen Street past last cottage

Local facilities
Market Weston, Hopton

Walking conditions
Good

Dogs
On lead only

Best time to visit
April–Oct

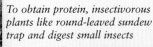

To obtain protein, insectivorous plants like round-leaved sundew trap and digest small insects

MARTIN'S MEADOWS

"First class. Ancient meadow flowers give this site a Shakespearean quality."

These three small meadows are among the few flower-rich hay meadows still left in Suffolk. As they have never been fertilised, sprayed or drained, the site is brimming with wildflowers. To make sure it stays this way, the meadows are managed by taking a hay cut in July and grazing the late summer growth in autumn.

In spring and early summer visitors can enjoy superb displays of wildflowers, including early-purple, green-winged and pyramidal orchids. Cowslips are plentiful and the rare snake's head fritillary can be found in the damper areas. In autumn the meadows bloom once more, this time with meadow saffron - a plant associated with ancient grasslands.

The hedges enclosing the site are hundreds of years old and contain many different species of trees and shrubs including field maple, hazel, hawthorn and spindle. They are maintained by coppicing, in which sections are periodically cut to the ground, encouraging them to regrow to produce a dense, long living hedge.

STAR SPECIES
Meadow saffron

Green-winged & Pyramidal orchids

Rare meadow saffron flowers in autumn

Two small orchards have been restored and planted with local varieties of fruit trees including apple, plum, pear and medlar.

Other Trust reserves nearby: Fox Fritillary Meadow

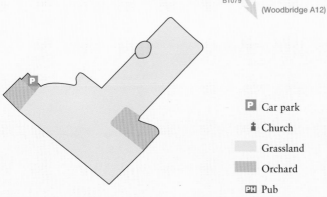

P Car park

✝ Church

   Grassland

   Orchard

PH Pub

Map
OS Landranger 156

Grid reference
TM 228572

Size
3.9 hectares (9.75 acres)

Status
SSSI

Parking
At entrance but please
don't block the gate

Local facilities
Otley

Walking conditions
Wet except in summer

Dogs
On leads only

Best time to visit
April–June, Sept

*Local varieties of apple
grow in the old orchard*

MELLIS COMMON

"The largest grazing common in Suffolk and fantastically flower-rich."

Areas of Mellis Common are literally strewn with wildflowers having been farmed by the common rights-holders for centuries, using traditional hay cutting and grazing. The Trust continues to manage it in the same way today to ensure the blooms and wildlife diversity remain. In summer rare plants such as green-winged orchid, sulphur clover and adder's tongue fern flourish. The abundance of small mammals also makes the site a favourite hunting ground for barn owl and tawny owl.

In stark contrast, the western end of the Common is botanically poorer due to the fact that it was ploughed and farmed more intensively during World War II. Since medieval times Mellis Common has been used as a source of clay for building, and is renowned for its ponds and wet depressions which add to the variety of plant and animal life. Some ponds support the nationally rare great-crested newt.

Management is underway to improve habitats that have declined over the years. Old pollarded trees and overgrown hedges have been cut to prolong their life and silted-up and overgrown ponds have been dredged to boost their wildlife value.

Adder's tongue fern

A striking jagged crest runs along the back of the great-crested newt. It has become rarer due to the infilling of ponds

STAR SPECIES

Adder's tongue fern

Green-winged orchid

Mellis Common was generously donated by Lord Henniker to Suffolk Wildlife Trust in 1989. Part of the Common is privately owned.

Other Trust reserves nearby: Redgrave & Lopham Fen, Thelnetham Fen, Wortham Ling

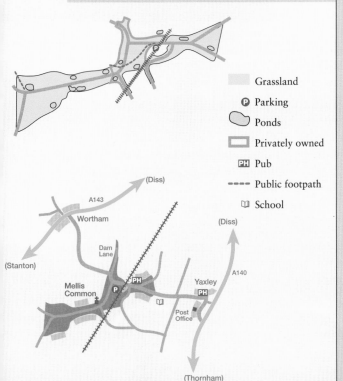

Grassland

P Parking

Ponds

Privately owned

PH Pub

---- Public footpath

School

Map
OS Landranger 144

Grid reference
TM 101746

Size
64.4 hectares (161 acres)

Status
CWS

Parking
Next to railway line

Local facilities
Local pub

Walking conditions
Soft even in summer

Access
During grazing electric fencing encloses some areas. Please don't walk on the Common when the grass is tall as this will damage the hay crop.

Dogs
Under control please

Best time to visit
May–July

THE MERE, FRAMLINGHAM

"A stroll around the stunningly beautiful Mere, combined with a visit to the bustling market town and medieval castle, makes this a great day out."

With its surrounding wet meadows and ancient castle backdrop, the Mere at Framlingham is considered by many to be the best view in inland Suffolk. Its wildlife is equally special and the reserve is best known for its sedge beds – a rare habitat in Suffolk – and stream of migrating birds. There is a wonderful show of massed marsh marigolds, delicate ragged-robin and lady's smock in spring and if water levels aren't too high, birds like green and common sandpiper and snipe can sometimes be seen.

A build up of silt over recent years resulted in restoration work being carried out by Suffolk Wildlife Trust, Framlingham College and the Environment Agency. This involved removing over 40,000 tonnes of accumulated mud from the Mere to restore water levels and wetland wildlife, pollarding historic trees and planting new ones and improving information for visitors. Wildlife has already responded to the improvement in water quality resulting from the restoration.

The Mere is cared for by Suffolk Wildlife Trust on behalf of Framlingham College.

Other Trust reserves nearby: Blythe Meadow

STAR SPECIES

Marsh marigold

Yellow flag iris

Snipe

Green sandpiper winter on lakes and marshes

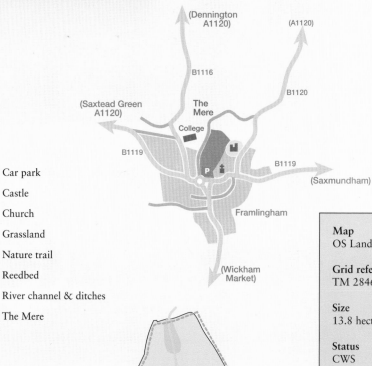

(Dennington A1120)

(A1120)

B1116

B1120

(Saxtead Green A1120)

The Mere

College

B1119

B1119

(Saxmundham)

P Car park

🏰 Castle

⛪ Church

Grassland

------ Nature trail

Reedbed

River channel & ditches

The Mere

Framlingham

(Wickham Market)

Framlingham Castle

Map
OS Landranger 156

Grid reference
TM 284638

Size
13.8 hectares (34.5 acres)

Status
CWS

Parking
Elms car park
next to Mere

Local facilities
Framlingham

Walking conditions
Often wet and boggy

Dogs
On leads only

Best time to visit
April–July

Yellow flag iris flowers between May and July

MICKFIELD MEADOW

"A rare jewel in an arable agricultural landscape."

Mickfield Meadow – which became Suffolk's first nature reserve in 1923 – is a stunning flower-rich hay meadow that has never been sprayed or fertilised. As a result it contains a host of wildflowers many of which are now scarce in Suffolk. To maintain this rich flora, the meadow is managed in the traditional way by taking a hay cut in July and then grazing the late summer growth in the autumn.

The unusual mix of plants growing here adds to its botanical interest. In parts of the meadow you can see goldilocks buttercup and the low growing wood anemone – both plants more usually associated with ancient woodlands. In the wetter parts look for marshland flowers like ragged-robin, meadowsweet and the beautiful snake's head fritillary – one of only four sites in Suffolk where it can still be found.

The boundary hedges are maintained by the traditional method of coppicing. This involves periodically cutting sections to the ground, which encourages regrowth and creates a long living, dense hedge that is great for wildlife.

STAR SPECIES

Snake's head fritillary

Goldilocks buttercup

Other Trust reserves nearby: Fox Fritillary Meadow

The snake's head fritillary's purple chequered bell-shaped flowers used to be seen in Suffolk's river valleys

Goldilocks buttercup

(Diss)

Wetherup Street

Mickfield Hall tradesmen entrance

Mickfield Meadow

A140

Mickfield Hall

Greenwood Farm

Watergarden Centre

Mickfield

Little Stonham

Stonham Aspal

(Stowmarket)

(Yoxford)

Earl Stonham

A1120

(A14)

P Car park

† Church

PH Pub

△ Radio mast

(Telephone

---- Track

Map
OS Landranger 156

Grid reference
TM 143633

Size
1.7 hectares (4.25 acres)

Status
SSSI

Parking
Limited to roadside

Local facilities
Mickfield

Walking conditions
Can be wet

Access
Around meadow margins only

Dogs
On leads only

Best time to visit
April, May

Ragged-robin

NACTON MEADOWS

"A fabulous piece of old England sunk between uniform arable farmland – a real treasure."

This delightful reserve is one of the last remnants of wet meadow in the Orwell Valley. The first meadow leads steeply down to a vale of wet grassland. This area of the valley bottom is best for wildflowers – rushes and meadowsweet bloom together with less common plants such as lesser spearwort, water figwort and breathtaking carpets of marsh marigold. In spring the show of southern marsh and common spotted orchid is spectacular and primeval forests of the strange, great horsetail which grows up to one and a half metres high, dwarf the smaller marsh horsetail.

The stream running along the meadow's edge is rich in invertebrates and as a result hosts a thriving frog and toad population. It's not unusual for grass snake to be seen here too, no doubt hunting down an amphibious snack.

The wealth of flowering plants attracts many insects including hoverfly, damselfly and dragonfly. Alder scrub provides good nesting and roosting areas for a variety of birds including winter visiting redpoll, siskin and chattering flocks of feeding goldfinch.

Nacton Meadows is cared for by Suffolk Wildlife Trust on behalf of the Orwell Estate.

STAR SPECIES

Southern marsh & Common spotted orchid

Other Trust reserves nearby: Levington Lagoon, Newbourne Springs

Male redpoll can be identified by their crimson crown and black bib

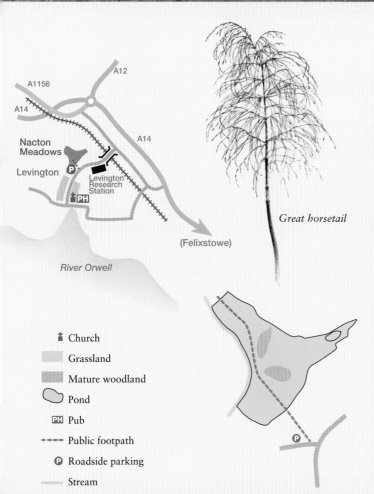

A12

A1156

A14

Nacton
Meadows

Levington

A14

Levington
Research
Station

PH

(Felixstowe)

River Orwell

Great horsetail

P

Map
OS Landranger 169

Grid reference
TM 232399

Size
3.5 hectares (8.75 acres)

Status
SSSI

Parking
Limited on roadside

Local facilities
Local pub nearby

Walking conditions
Damp

Dogs
On leads only

Best time to visit
April–Aug

Church

Grassland

Mature woodland

Pond

PH Pub

Public footpath

P Roadside parking

Stream

NEWBOURNE SPRINGS

"The woodland is like a secret garden where you instinctively tip-toe round corners and talk in hushed tones."

This small wooded valley with its spring-fed stream used to be a source of water for Felixstowe. Together with its small area of marsh, fen and adjacent heathland this reserve is good for flowering plants and a variety of birds including nuthatch, treecreeper, goldcrest and all three kinds of woodpecker. Butterfly include the speckled wood and green hairstreak while the dancing lights of glow worm are sometimes spotted during balmy summer nights.

STAR SPECIES

Nightingale

Marsh marigold

This site is an SSSI because of the sheer variety of habitats and associated wildlife. Evocative nightingale song characterises the reserve in spring when you can find water avens and spectacular displays of marsh marigold alongside the stream. Careful scrutiny will also reveal common twayblade and the more open areas are covered in common spotted orchid. The woodland is dominated by oak, ash, alder, hazel and hawthorn.

A marked trail takes you around the reserve and a leaflet is available from the visitor centre.

Newbourne Springs is cared for by Suffolk Wildlife Trust on behalf of Anglian Water.

Other Trust reserves nearby: Nacton Meadow

Nightingale have a beautiful, musical song

Legend:

- P — Car park/visitor centre
- Fen meadow
- Heath
- Mature woodland
- ---- Nature trail
- Pond
- PH — Pub
- Scrub

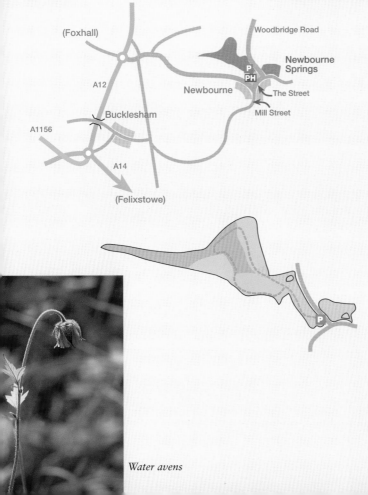

(Foxhall)

Woodbridge Road

Newbourne Springs

A12

Newbourne

P PH

The Street

Bucklesham

Mill Street

A1156

A14

(Felixstowe)

P

Water avens

Map
OS Landranger 169

Grid reference
TM 273435

Size
13 hectares (32.5 acres)

Status
SSSI, Visitor centre

Parking
Small car park at the junction of Woodbridge Road & The Street

Local facilities
Local pub opposite

Walking conditions
Can be wet, uneven and steep in places

Dogs
On leads only

Best time to visit
April–July

NORAH HANBURY-KELK
Meadows

NORAH HANBURY-KELK
MEADOWS

"My grandfather hired these meadows to graze his cattle and horses in the 1940s. They are as colourful now as I remember them from my childhood."

Norah Hanbury-Kelk Meadows are a network of small, flower-rich wet meadows and are probably one of the best inland sites in Suffolk for breeding waders such as snipe, lapwing and redshank.

The high water levels, vital for wetland wildlife, are controlled by a system of dams and ditches. In summer the meadows are cut or grazed to maintain the rich variety of wetland plants such as ragged-robin, lady's smock, greater bird's-foot trefoil and both early and southern marsh orchid.

The pale early marsh orchid is one of the first to flower. Although similar to the southern marsh orchid, it is much scarcer. The number of orchids has increased significantly since the Trust acquired the meadows and reintroduced grazing and water level management in 1980.

Listen too for the drumming of displaying male snipe as they swoop across the meadows and the flute-like notes of male redshank. The reserve is closed from mid-March to July to protect these ground nesting birds, but they can easily be seen from the footpath along the meadow's edge.

Snipe

Other Trust reserves nearby:
Lackford Lakes, Rex Graham

Redshank incubating eggs

STAR SPECIES

Early marsh orchid

Snipe

Redshank

Suffolk Wildlife Trust is grateful to the Hanbury-Kelk family who generously donated the meadows in 1980.

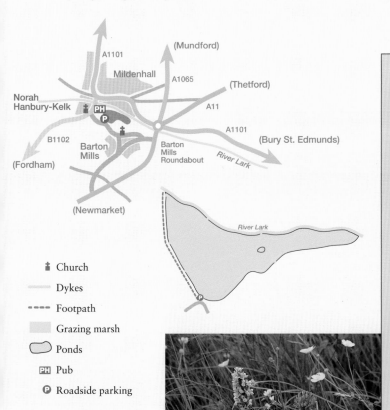

Key:

- ⛪ Church
- ── Dykes
- ---- Footpath
- ▨ Grazing marsh
- ⬭ Ponds
- PH Pub
- Ⓟ Roadside parking

In summer, a riot of wildflowers makes this meadow a delight

Map
OS Landranger 143

Grid reference
TL 713740

Size
7.8 hectares (19.5 acres)

Status
CWS

Parking
Limited space by entrance

Local facilities
Bell Inn, Barton Mills

Walking conditions
Damp/wet in winter

Access
No access Mar–July, view from adjacent footpath

Dogs
Sorry no dogs, sensitive site

Best time to view
March–July

NORTH COVE

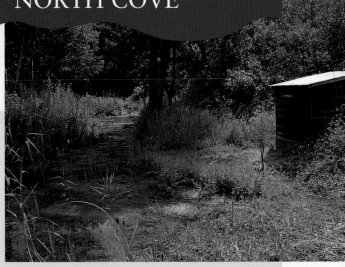

"There's so much to see and hear. Just find a spot, sit, soak in the atmosphere and let the wildlife come to you!"

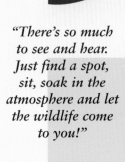

North Cove is a quiet relaxing place with a patchwork of wetland habitats including grazing marsh, wet woodland and pools, all lying in the valley of the River Waveney. Characteristic marshland plants like ragged-robin and yellow rattle (so named because the dried seeds rattle in their pods) have become established along with nationally scarce marsh fern which is thriving here. Bog pimpernel occurs in the meadow and opposite-leaved golden saxifrage can be found near the old decoy pond.

The mature woodland is good for birds like warbler, siskin, redpoll and all three types of woodpecker. Nightingale and woodcock nest in the scrub and young carr while sparrow-hawk can often be seen hunting, their swift swooping flight low to the ground.

Pools and dykes attract many kinds of dragonfly including the Norfolk hawker. Smooth newt and the ten-spined stickleback also occur. In summer grass snake and common lizard soak up the sun in warm sheltered areas.

STAR SPECIES

Norfolk hawker dragonfly

Woodcock

Woodcock have perfected the art of camouflage

To maintain this wonderful array of wildlife, cattle are used to graze the meadows, encroaching scrub is kept at bay, the old decoy pond is regularly cleared and the summerhouse ride mown.

North Cove is cared for by Suffolk Wildlife Trust on behalf of a private owner.

Other Trust reserves nearby: Carlton Marshes, Castle Marshes, Oulton Marshes

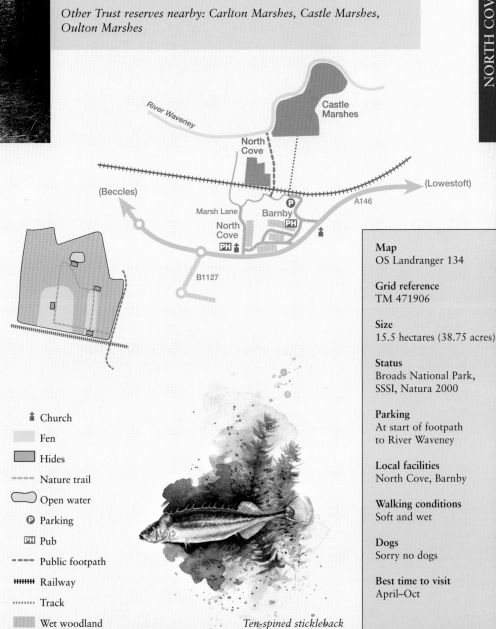

Castle Marshes

River Waveney

North Cove

(Beccles)

Marsh Lane

Barnby
PH

North Cove
PH

(Lowestoft)

A146

B1127

Map
OS Landranger 134

Grid reference
TM 471906

Size
15.5 hectares (38.75 acres)

Status
Broads National Park, SSSI, Natura 2000

Parking
At start of footpath to River Waveney

Local facilities
North Cove, Barnby

Walking conditions
Soft and wet

Dogs
Sorry no dogs

Best time to visit
April–Oct

- Church
- Fen
- Hides
- Nature trail
- Open water
- Parking
- Pub
- Public footpath
- Railway
- Track
- Wet woodland

Ten-spined stickleback

OULTON MARSHES

"A tapestry of different habitats and part of a once extensive Broadland landscape."

Oulton Marshes is a jigsaw of short fen meadow, tall litter fen, dykes, pools and scrub. Mostly man-made, these habitats have developed over hundreds of years of traditional management and now host specialised wildlife.

The fen meadows lie on top of deep layers of waterlogged peat and support many rare plants. In early summer there is a fabulous display of southern marsh orchid, marsh marigold and ragged-robin, together with the scarcer bogbean, bog pimpernel and marsh cinquefoil.

The taller fen contains plants such as marsh pea and marsh sowthistle that are rare outside the Broads. Breeding birds like grasshopper, reed and sedge warbler and the rare Cetti's warbler have also settled in.

The network of dykes which divide the marshes are full of aquatic wildlife and are noted for dragonfly and damselfly. The margins support a range of wetland plants including brookweed, arrowhead and purple loosestrife.

STAR SPECIES

Marsh pea

Grasshopper & Cetti's warbler

The sedge warbler can be identified by its pale eye stripe

The reserve is managed through a combination of mowing and grazing. Scrub and dyke clearance is carried out regularly to maintain the open fen habitat and waterways.

Much of the reserve is too wet for public access, but can be comfortably viewed from the Fisher Row footpath which runs alongside. One of the marshes, Robinson's Marsh, was purchased by the Trust as a result of a legacy by Mrs Ruth Robinson.

Other Trust reserves nearby: Camps Heath, Carlton Marshes, Castle Marshes, Foxburrow Wood, North Cove

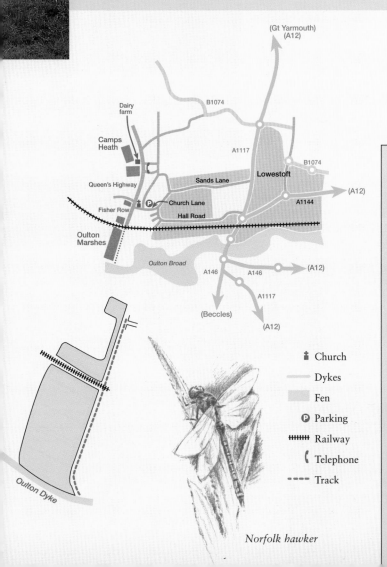

Church

Dykes

Fen

Parking

Railway

Telephone

Track

Norfolk hawker

Map
OS Landranger 134

Grid reference
TM 505934

Size
15.75 hectares (39.4 acres)

Status
CWS, Broads National Park

Parking
By Oulton Church,
Church Lane

Local facilities
Oulton

Walking conditions
Muddy in winter/spring

Dogs
On lead only

Best time to visit
April–July

PASHFORD POORS FEN

"A quiet spot with amazing variety; lots of individual pockets to explore, each with their different wildlife."

This spring fed fen with herb-rich meadows was allocated to the poor in 1679 for grazing and peat digging. More recently management has focused on conserving the flower-studded grassland by the use of grazing cattle. Chalk grassland plants include quaking grass, cowslip, small scabious, sheep's bit and Devil's-bit scabious. In the fen area plants such as marsh marigold, bugle, ragged-robin, saw sedge, yellow sedge and greater burnet provide a splash of colour.

Brimstone and speckled wood butterfly and a large variety of moths have been recorded here including some specific to Breckland. The fen is also the only known site in Britain for the rare leaf beetle *Cryptocephalus exiguus*, about which little is known except that the young appear to feed on sorrel. Precise control of stock grazing is needed to manage its habitat. Birds such as whitethroat, treecreeper and long-tailed tit nest in the small woodland where roe deer are regularly seen.

STAR SPECIES

Greater burnet

Roe deer

Small scabious

Long-tailed tit build delicate, globe-shaped nests

The fen has been threatened by drainage of surrounding land. However in 1996 the SSSI boundary was expanded to extend control over nearby drainage ditches and new banks were installed to keep water levels high.

Pashford Poors Fen is leased by Suffolk Wildlife Trust from Lakenheath Consolidated Charities.

Other Trust reserves nearby: Brandon Artemisia, Lakenheath Poors Fen, Wangford Warren

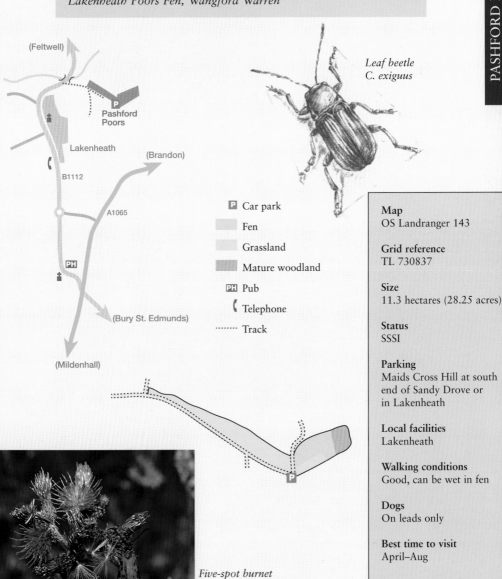

*Leaf beetle
C. exiguus*

(Feltwell)

Pashford
Poors

Lakenheath

(Brandon)

B1112

A1065

(Bury St. Edmunds)

(Mildenhall)

P Car park

Fen

Grassland

Mature woodland

PH Pub

(Telephone

········· Track

Map
OS Landranger 143

Grid reference
TL 730837

Size
11.3 hectares (28.25 acres)

Status
SSSI

Parking
Maids Cross Hill at south end of Sandy Drove or in Lakenheath

Local facilities
Lakenheath

Walking conditions
Good, can be wet in fen

Dogs
On leads only

Best time to visit
April–Aug

Five-spot burnet moth on thistle

REDGRAVE & LOPHAM FEN

"Visitors new to the Fen are astounded when they find out about its recent history. The open landscape gives a rare sense of space and people comment on the primeval feel to the site."

This is the largest remaining river valley fen in England and the source of the River Waveney. As one of the most important wetlands in Europe, Redgrave and Lopham Fen now has international protection. As well as open fen the reserve includes a mixture of wet heathland, open water, scrub and woodland. The underlying acid and alkaline geology has resulted in characteristic wildlife including many species now rare in Britain.

Historically local people dug peat for fuel, harvested reed and sedge for thatching and grazed the drier margins with cattle. With the demise of these activities, together with post-war drainage and water abstraction, the fen began to dry out and degrade.

The Trust's restoration project has included the reinstatement of traditional management, grazing with a herd of resilient Polish tarpan ponies, cattle and sheep, peat scraping to expose fresh wet peat and the re-siting of a public water abstraction borehole. This has resulted in rehydration of the fen and the gradual return of its wonderful wildlife. Already wetland species such as butterwort, marsh fragrant orchid and cross-leaved heath have made a comeback as have breeding snipe.

STAR SPECIES
Fen raft spider

Saw sedge

Butterwort

Tarpan ponies, a tough breed from Poland play a vital role in conserving the fen

Emerald damselfly used to be known as 'Devil's darning needles'. Damselfly are smaller and more slender than dragonfly – neither insect stings

Cross-leaved heath

REDGRAVE & LOPHAM FEN

Fen raft spider sit on floating vegetation waiting to ambush prey such as stickleback and tadpole

Reed and sedge beds dominate and play host to a variety of insects, which in turn attract insect-eating birds like grasshopper warbler and reed bunting. The chalkier sedge beds feature a range of wetland plants including meadowsweet, ragged-robin, greater spearwort and black bog rush. Areas are mown at different times to create a mixed habitat which attracts birds such as snipe. The small pools – a legacy of ancient peat diggers – are now home to the elegant fen raft spider found in only one other area in the UK. Water vole can be seen in the sedge beds and along the river together with otter and kingfisher.

In the more acidic conditions at the western end of the fen heathland plants thrive. Many rare species including insectivorous butterwort can be seen here and adder and lizard often bask in the sun.

Redgrave and Lopham Fen is cared for by Suffolk Wildlife Trust and owned by the Trust and various Poors Charities.

Other Trust reserves nearby: Hopton Fen, Market Weston Fen, Mellis Common, Thelnetham Fen, Wortham Ling

A typical spider pool

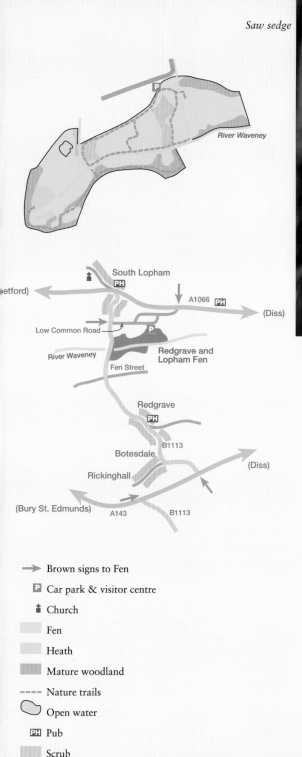

Saw sedge

South Lopham
PH
(etford)
A1066 PH
(Diss)
Low Common Road
P
River Waveney
Redgrave and
Lopham Fen
Fen Street
Redgrave
PH
Botesdale
B1113
(Diss)
Rickinghall
(Bury St. Edmunds)
A143   B1113

REDGRAVE & LOPHAM FEN

→ Brown signs to Fen

P Car park & visitor centre

⛪ Church

▭ Fen

▭ Heath

▭ Mature woodland

---- Nature trails

⬭ Open water

PH Pub

▭ Scrub

Map
OS Landranger 144

Grid reference
TM 052801

Size
123 hectares (307.5 acres)

Status
SSSI, NNR, Natura 2000,
RAMSAR, Education
and visitor centre

Parking
On-site car park

Local facilities
Loos and snacks at visitor centre

Walking conditions
Can be muddy

Dogs
On leads only

Wheelchair/pushchair
Accessible boardwalk

Best time to visit
April–Sept

REYDON WOOD

"In late spring bluebells carpet the floor; the song of the nightingale is the sweetest of all the birds."

Reydon Wood is a typical Suffolk ancient woodland with features characteristic of medieval coppice wood. The southern boundary consists of an impressive bank and ditch. In the wood itself there are many large coppice stools, some hundreds of years old.

Centuries of coppicing – the traditional way of havesting wood – have allowed sunlight to regularly flood the woodland floor resulting in a unique ground flora. To encourage this spectacular show of spring flowers the Trust is continuing coppice management and gradually removing planted conifers. Look out for early-purple orchid, violet, twayblade, primrose and yellow archangel that flourish in the newly cut areas.

The wood is enriched by a network of rides that have been widened to create sun-drenched, grassy glades enjoyed by butterflies such as ringlet, gatekeeper, orange tip, speckled wood and painted lady. These open tracks are particularly rich in wildflowers with common spotted orchid, ragged-robin and fleabane in abundance.

STAR SPECIES

Bluebell

Common spotted & Early-purple orchid

Birds to look out for include tawny owl, sparrowhawk, long-tailed tit, woodcock and treecreeper.

Sparrowhawk are agile woodland predators

In spring, listen for blackcap and nightingale singing in the more recently coppiced areas.

Other Trust reserves nearby: Hen Reedbed, Wenhaston Commons

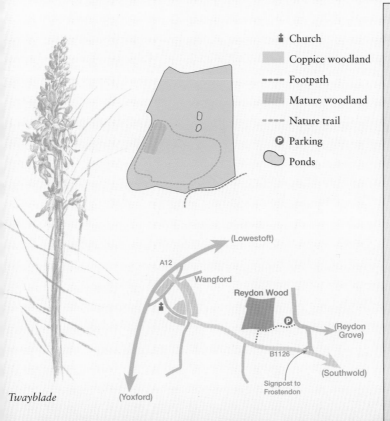

Key

✝ Church

▨ Coppice woodland

---- Footpath

▨ Mature woodland

---- Nature trail

🅿 Parking

⬭ Ponds

(Lowestoft)

A12

Wangford

Reydon Wood

🅿

(Reydon Grove)

B1126

(Southwold)

Signpost to Frostenden

(Yoxford)

Twayblade

Map
OS Landranger 156

Grid reference
TM 476788

Size
16 hectares (40 acres)

Status
CWS

Parking
Limited, at end of track leading to reserve

Local facilities
Wangford

Walking conditions
Firm/wet after rain

Dogs
On leads only

Best time to visit
April, May

SIMPSON'S SALTINGS

"A wonderfully lonely and isolated spot with an aura of timelessness."

For some, the immediate appeal of Simpson's Saltings is its openness and wide views of the Ore estuary. It is also one of the county's most important coastal sites for its wealth of uncommon coastal and saltmarsh plants. *(For this reason the Saltings can only be viewed from the sea wall.)*

These plants grow amongst a mosaic of habitats including compacted sand, shingle, saltmarsh, inter-tidal mud and estuary creeks. Sea campion, thrift and bird's-foot trefoil flourish here alongside many rarer plants such as sea kale, sea pea and sea heath. Rare and fragile lichens too, have developed in the absence of trampling feet.

Inter-tidal mud provides rich pickings for wading birds, while areas of sand and shingle make ideal nesting sites for ringed plover and oystercatcher. Little and common tern are a regular sight and during the autumn and winter migrations, wheatear and flocks of meadow pipit swell the numbers.

The reserve was generously purchased for Suffolk Wildlife Trust by Francis Simpson – a well known Suffolk botanist – with additional support from English Nature.

Other Trust reserves nearby: Sutton & Hollesley Commons

STAR SPECIES

Sea heath

Sea pea

Oystercatcher probe the mud for juicy morsels and prize shellfish open with their chisel-like beaks

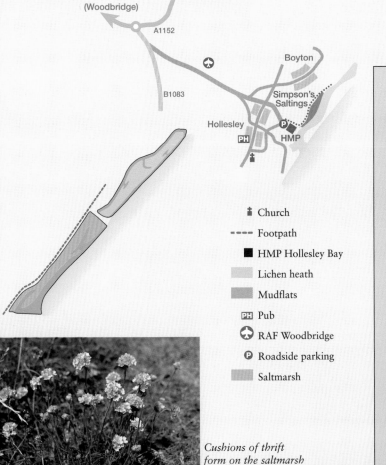

(Woodbridge)

A1152

Boyton

B1083

Simpson's
Saltings

Hollesley

P

PH   HMP

✝

✝	Church
----	Footpath
■	HMP Hollesley Bay
	Lichen heath
	Mudflats
PH	Pub
✈	RAF Woodbridge
P	Roadside parking
	Saltmarsh

*Cushions of thrift
form on the saltmarsh*

Map
OS Landranger 169

Grid reference
TM 385455

Size
15 hectares (37.5 acres)

Status
SSSI, Natura 2000

Parking
HMP Hollesley Bay

Local facilities
Hollesley, Butley

Access
No picnics or landing
boats due to fragile
plants

Walking conditions
Can be wet and uneven

Dogs
On lead only

Best time to visit
May–Aug

SIZEWELL BELTS

"A secluded landscape of grazing marsh intersected by a series of dykes and tree belts – a good example of how industry and conservation can work together."

Marsh, reedbed and wet woodland with adjacent heathland and beach - Sizewell Belts has just about everything! This diverse site is one of the best wetlands in East Anglia for wildflowers; it is a stronghold for otter, water vole and kingfisher, whilst water rail and barn owl can often be seen. The rare and haunting bittern and flighty bearded tit are also found here.

The wildflower meadows, which are maintained by cattle and sheep grazing, include four species of orchid, yellow rattle, ragged-robin, bogbean and lady's smock. In summer the dykes are alive with many dragonfly (17 species have been recorded) including hairy and migrant hawker dragonfly. Visiting birds like wigeon, snipe and shoveler are attracted to the flooded marshes during winter.

Barn owl

Leaflets detailing walks on Sizewell Belts and the adjacent Kenton and Goose Hills are available in the car park.

Sizewell Belts is cared for by Suffolk Wildlife Trust on behalf of British Energy.

Other Trust reserves nearby: Darsham Marshes, The Haven Thorpeness, Hazelwood Marshes

STAR SPECIES
Otter

Water vole

Barn owl

Otter are now starting to reappear on many of our rivers

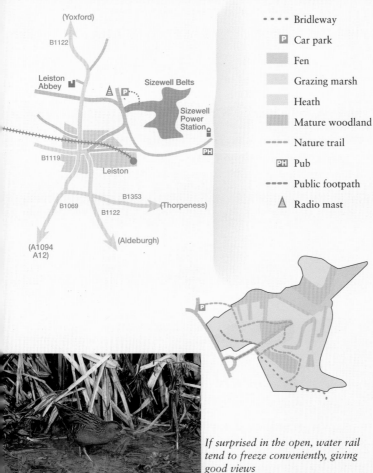

Legend

- - - - Bridleway
- P Car park
- Fen
- Grazing marsh
- Heath
- Mature woodland
- - - - - Nature trail
- PH Pub
- - - - - Public footpath
- ⚠ Radio mast

Map
OS Landranger 156

Grid reference
TM 454638

Size
94.5 hectares (236.25 acres)

Status
SSSI

Parking
Kenton Hills car park
off Lovers' Lane

Local facilities
Local café and pub

Walking conditions
Good, marsh wet in winter

Dogs
Sorry no dogs

Wheelchair/pushchair
Access to woodlands

Best time to visit
May–July

If surprised in the open, water rail tend to freeze conveniently, giving good views

SPOUSE'S VALE

"In an hour's walk you get it all: wet alder woodland, dry oak and hazel, wet meadow and the fens."

Spouse's Vale is a fascinating mosaic of ancient woodland alongside fen meadow. The interesting mix of trees includes oak, ash, field maple, holly and crab apple with some wild cherry, superb large alder and old hazel. It's best to visit in spring when you will be greeted with a fabulous show of bluebell accompanied by the magical song of nightingale. You may also be lucky enough to flush a woodcock from the undergrowth.

Butterfly to look out for include the speckled wood, meadow brown, orange tip, holly blue and comma. Common lizard and grass snake bask in the summer sun and in winter flocks of siskin can be an unexpected pleasure. Roe deer and fox are often seen. Survey work has revealed the presence of the yellow-necked mouse and rare dormouse here.

The meadows are kept wet by spring flushes on the mid slopes. Here sandy gravels meet peat, making them ideal for wetland plants such as purple loosestrife as well as broad-bodied chaser dragonfly, frog and toad.

STAR SPECIES

Bluebell

Nightingale

A fox's diet includes insects, eggs and fruit as well as small mammals

Suffolk Wildlife Trust is restoring the meadows at Spouse's Vale to their former glory through a careful programme of scrub clearance, mowing and grazing.

Misses Edith and Frances Vale generously purchased this reserve for Suffolk Wildlife Trust.

Other Trust reserves nearby: Cornard Mere

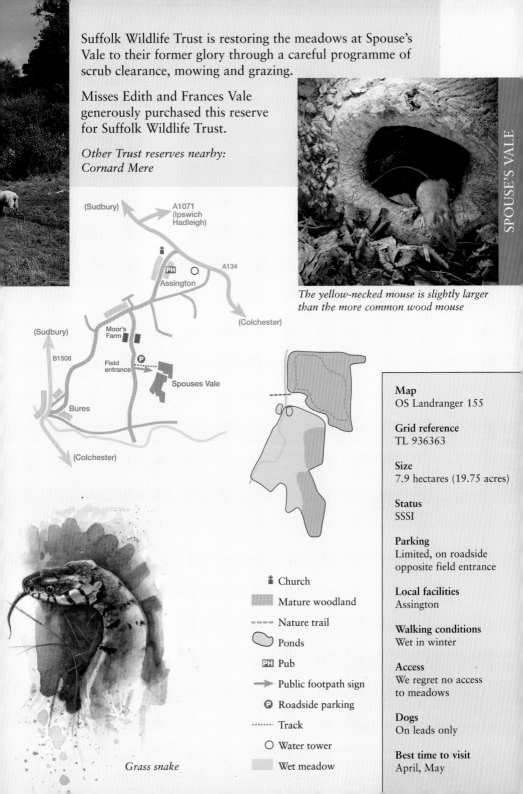

SPOUSE'S VALE

The yellow-necked mouse is slightly larger than the more common wood mouse

(Sudbury)

A1071 (Ipswich Hadleigh)

A134

Assington

(Colchester)

(Sudbury)

Moor's Farm

B1508

Field entrance

Spouses Vale

Bures

(Colchester)

Map
OS Landranger 155

Grid reference
TL 936363

Size
7.9 hectares (19.75 acres)

Status
SSSI

Parking
Limited, on roadside opposite field entrance

Local facilities
Assington

Walking conditions
Wet in winter

Access
We regret no access to meadows

Dogs
On leads only

Best time to visit
April, May

ⓘ	Church
	Mature woodland
----	Nature trail
⬭	Ponds
PH	Pub
→	Public footpath sign
Ⓟ	Roadside parking
......	Track
O	Water tower
	Wet meadow

Grass snake

SUTTON & HOLLESLEY COMMONS

"The fluting song of woodlark; the intensity of purple heather; the spooky churring of nightjar on a summer's night – heathland heaven!"

These heaths represent one of the largest continuous areas of Sandlings heath left and are at their most colourful in August and September. Mature Scots pine and birch mix with gorse, heather and bracken to produce a fabulous place for wildlife. Birds like stonechat, nightjar, woodlark, redstart, tree pipit and winter visitors like hen harrier, crossbill and flocks of finch, provide interest all year round.

This is one of the few sites for the delicate silver-studded blue butterfly. Species such as green tiger beetle, adder, fallow deer and pipistrelle, long-eared and noctule bat combine to give this heathland added appeal.

To conserve habitat diversity from open heathland to woodland, these heaths are regularly cut and grazed by Suffolk Wildlife Trust's own sheep flock to keep invasive bracken and scrub at bay.

This site has good public facilities with car parks, picnic areas and nature trails.

Managed by Suffolk Wildlife Trust in partnership with Suffolk Coastal District Council, the Broxtead Estate and registered commoners.

Other Trust reserves nearby: Simpson's Saltings, Bromeswell Green

STAR SPECIES

Nightjar

Long-eared bat

Silver-studded blue butterfly

Long-eared bats roost in buildings and trees

Silver-studded blue butterfly

SUTTON & HOLLESLEY COMMONS

P Car park

Conifer woodland

Heath

---- Paths & nature trail

PH Pub

⊕ RAF Woodbridge

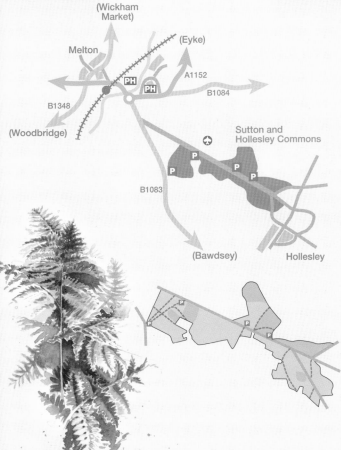

(Wickham Market)

Melton

(Eyke)

A1152

PH **PH**

B1084

B1348

(Woodbridge)

Sutton and Hollesley Commons

⊕

P

P **P**

P

B1083

(Bawdsey)

Hollesley

P

P

P

Bracken

Map
OS Landranger 169

Grid reference
TM 350465

Size
440 hectares (1,100 acres)

Status
SSSI, Natura 2000

Parking
Sutton Heath & Upper
Hollesley Common car parks

Walking conditions
Mostly dry & firm

Dogs
On leads only

Local facilities
Melton, Sutton, Hollesley

Wheelchair/pushchair
Reasonable access along trails

Best time to visit
April–Sept

THELNETHAM FEN

"Stand still, close your eyes and listen to the whispering of the fen..."

These small valley fens have survived the threat of nearby dredging of the Little Ouse River and are havens for water-loving plants. Both Old Fen and Middle Fen are dominated by a mix of saw sedge and black bog rush, with shows of grass-of-Parnassus in the calcium-rich spring flushes. Marsh lousewort grows here along with stonewort – an interesting algae whose skeleton can be seen in pools amongst the sedge.

Old Fen is now mainly alder carr and has dried out to some extent, but the mixed sedge fen in the middle is bursting with wild flowers. Breeding birds include snipe, with its drumming mating display, and grasshopper warbler, identified by its reeling song.

Open fen areas are cared for by mowing and scrub removal. Thelnetham Fen is cared for by Suffolk Wildlife Trust on behalf of Thelnetham Foeffe.

Other Trust reserves nearby: Hopton Fen, Market Weston Fen, Redgrave & Lopham Fen

STAR SPECIES

Grass-of-Parnassus

Stonewort

Black bog rush

Grass-of-Parnassus

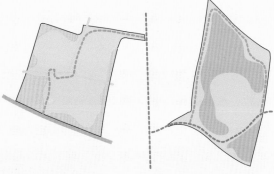

T. Andrewartha

Grasshopper warbler have a high pitched reeling song

🜊 Church

Fen

---- Footpath

Mature woodland

---- Nature trail

🅿 Parking

PH Pub

Scrub

✖ Windmill

Map
OS Landranger 144

Grid reference
TM 018785

Size
8.8 hectares (22 acres)

Status
SSSI, Natura 2000

Parking
Thelnetham village

Local facilities
Surrounding villages

Walking conditions
Can be muddy

Dogs
On leads only

Best time to visit
May–Aug

TRIMLEY MARSHES

"There are wonderful views of the Orwell estuary from here. An unbeatable wetland for its sheer number and species of birds."

Trimley Marshes is an exciting wetland reserve created almost entirely from arable land alongside the River Orwell. Most of the wildlife here today has colonised the site since it was created in 1990 to mitigate against the loss of Fagbury mudflats as a result of the expansion of the Port of Felixstowe.

The mosaic of habitats, managed primarily for birds, makes this reserve one of the best sites in the county. Many of the wet meadows are managed by the traditional method of grazing with cattle. Others are grazed with sheep and by wigeon and geese during the winter months.

STAR SPECIES
Avocet

Wigeon

Brent goose

Water levels are controlled by a system of sluices. This means that wet conditions can be maintained for wintering wildfowl including wigeon and brent goose and then for breeding waders such as redshank, avocet, oystercatcher and black-tailed godwit.

The reservoir is the hub of the reserve, acting not only as a refuge for wildfowl and marginal nesting birds, but also as the storage and distribution point for the reserve's water. Rafts of coot, tufted duck, teal and pochard mingling with cormorant, gadwall and shoveler, are a common sight here.

Shingle islands have been created to encourage breeding waders

Like all hawker dragonfly, the emperor spends most of its time hunting on the wing. Activity depends on temperature and on cloudy days, during early morning or evening they are often motionless

Avocet

TRIMLEY MARSHES

The lagoon and its islands provide a variety of habitats throughout the year. The islands are ideal nesting sites for avocet, ringed plover and tufted duck. In spring and autumn the muddy margins make excellent feeding grounds for migrating waders such as common sandpiper, curlew sandpiper and greenshank.

The network of dykes are mostly fringed with reed. Look out for little grebe, moorhen and both reed and sedge warbler, as well as Britain's largest hawker dragonfly, the emperor.

Trimley Marshes are leased to Suffolk Wildlife Trust by the Port of Felixstowe.

Other Trust reserves nearby: Landguard, Levington Lagoon

Ringed plover are among the birds that nest on the shingle island

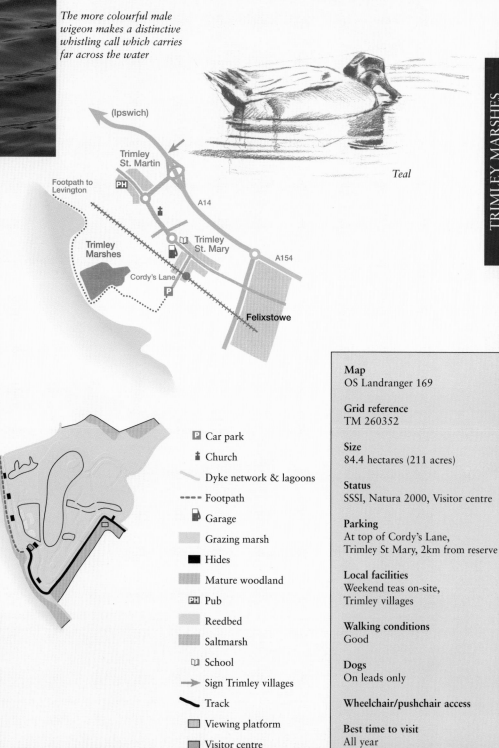

*The more colourful male
wigeon makes a distinctive
whistling call which carries
far across the water*

Teal

(Ipswich)

Trimley
St. Martin

PH

A14

Footpath to
Levington

Trimley
Marshes

Trimley
St. Mary

A154

Cordy's Lane

P

Felixstowe

P Car park

✝ Church

⁓ Dyke network & lagoons

---- Footpath

⛽ Garage

Grazing marsh

■ Hides

Mature woodland

PH Pub

Reedbed

Saltmarsh

📖 School

→ Sign Trimley villages

━ Track

☐ Viewing platform

Visitor centre

Map
OS Landranger 169

Grid reference
TM 260352

Size
84.4 hectares (211 acres)

Status
SSSI, Natura 2000, Visitor centre

Parking
At top of Cordy's Lane,
Trimley St Mary, 2km from reserve

Local facilities
Weekend teas on-site,
Trimley villages

Walking conditions
Good

Dogs
On leads only

Wheelchair/pushchair access

Best time to visit
All year

WANGFORD WARREN

"A living piece of Breckland history."

Wangford Warren is the best surviving example of a once extensive sand dune system. As its name suggests the site was originally used to rear rabbits and their grazing, along with sheep, still plays a crucial part in its conservation today. An evening visit is particularly rewarding with silver birch glowing pink in the setting sun, providing a contrast against the dunes and fast fading blue sky.

Breckland soils are a mix of glacial silt, sand and gravel which vary in both depth and acidity. When Neolithic people cleared the original woodland this light, mobile soil was exposed and has developed into an active dune system. Sand sedge now binds these dunes together but in many places the soil is so poor that little more than lichen and moss can grow.

STAR SPECIES
Breckland lichen
Woodlark

Open disturbed soils are an important feature of Breckland heaths and have resulted in a specialised range of plant and animal life, rare or absent elsewhere in Britain. Wangford Warren is the only inland UK site for the beautiful grey hair grass. Many other rarities occur including shepherd's cress, bearded fescue and reindeer moss lichens. Areas of open sand are important for rare spiders and insects which frequent Breckland.

Rabbit grazing helps create ideal conditions for Breckland flowers to thrive

Access is restricted between March and August due to the fragile nature of the habitat and the risk of disturbing ground nesting birds such as woodlark. Other birds to be seen include wheatear and whinchat.

To visit between March and August please contact Suffolk Wildlife Trust.

Other Trust reserves nearby: Brandon Artemisia, Lakenheath Poors Fen, Pashford Poors Fen

- Bracken
- Church
- Fen
- Heath
- Lakenheath airbase
- Mature woodland
- PH Pub
- P Roadside parking

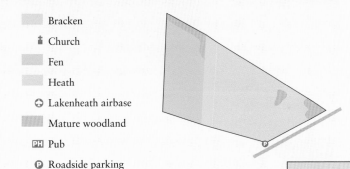

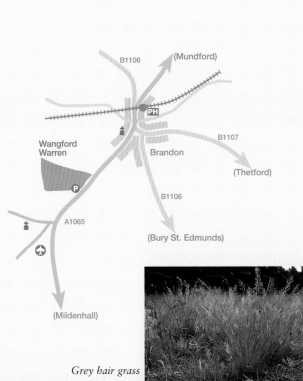

Grey hair grass

Map
OS Landranger 143

Grid reference
TL 756842

Size
14.6 hectares (36.5 acres)

Status
SSSI, Natura 2000

Parking
Limited, adjacent to main gate to reserve on A1065

Local facilities
Brandon

Access
Restricted March–August

Walking conditions
Good, always dry but watch out for rabbit holes!

Dogs
Sorry no dogs, sensitive site

Best time to visit
By appointment March–August

WENHASTON COMMONS

"There's no better way to spend an afternoon than exploring the rolling heaths and commons of Wenhaston, especially when gorse and the first flowering heathers are ablaze."

The five small interconnecting heaths of Wenhaston Commons include Blackheath, Mill Heath, Church Common, Bickers Heath and Blowers Common. The picturesque and quiet character of these sites belies the fact that, on closer inspection, they are teaming with wildlife.

During spring and early summer nightingale song drifts over the heaths. There is the stunning sight of bell heather and coconut-scented yellow gorse in bloom in mid June. In August amethyst shades of ling colour the scene.

Harebell, wood sage and heath bedstraw are amongst the wild flowers to be seen at Mill Heath. Tangles of honeysuckle, bramble and gorse characterise Blackheath whose ancient dew pond holds great-crested newt – best viewed by torchlight at night.

The Commons' many butterfly include the rare silver-studded blue. Lizard and slow worm, which being shy creatures will usually make off quickly as you approach, bask in sheltered sun traps and large, bright green tiger beetle scuttle haphazardly over the rough ground.

STAR SPECIES

Silver-studded blue butterfly

Woodlark

Bell heather

D. Jones

Long legged green tiger beetle are fast runners that fly off noisily if disturbed

Woodlark, whose stockier build and jerkier movements distinguish it from its skylark cousin, are also a speciality.

Wenhaston Commons are managed through a partnership between Suffolk Wildlife Trust, Suffolk Coastal District Council, a private owner and the Wenhaston Commons Management Group.

Other Trust reserves nearby: Hen Reedbed, Reydon Wood

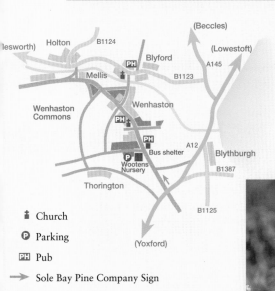

Church

P Parking

PH Pub

➜ Sole Bay Pine Company Sign

Bell heather is the first flowering of all the heathers

Map
OS Landranger 156

Grid reference
TM 422748

Size
26.25 hectares (65.6 acres)

Status
CWS

Parking
Wenhaston village

Local facilities
Wenhaston

Walking conditions
Dry & firm

Dogs
On leads only

Best time to visit
April–Sept

WINKS MEADOW

"Regular hay cutting keeps this tiny island of wildlife studded with wildflowers, providing a rare splash of colour in a sea of arable land."

Winks Meadow is a remnant of flower-rich grassland laden with wildflowers including the scarce spiny restharrow, sulphur clover and quaking grass. It has never been sprayed with pesticides or modern fertilisers, which is why it's so fabulous for plants.

Primrose and cowslip herald the start of this floral kaleidoscope in spring, while species normally associated with woodland such as dog's mercury and barren strawberry grow close to the hedges. Renowned for its spectacular displays of orchids, an awe-inspiring seven species grow here. The first to flower in late spring and early summer are twayblade, early-purple and green-winged orchid. Later in the summer common spotted, bee, and pyramidal orchid appear together with the only colony of frog orchid in Suffolk.

To make sure the meadow stays special, management involves either summer grazing with cattle or taking a hay cut in July, followed by autumn grazing. The hedge surrounding the meadow is a great wildlife habitat and there is a particularly fine stretch bordering the road. The many shrub species include spindle, field maple and dogwood, which suggest it is an ancient boundary.

STAR SPECIES

Green-winged & Frog orchid

Spiny restharrow

The bee orchid is convincingly like its namesake

The hedges are maintained by trimming or coppicing, which encourages dense regrowth.

Winks Meadow is owned and cared for by Suffolk Wildlife Trust. Plantlife generously supported its purchase.

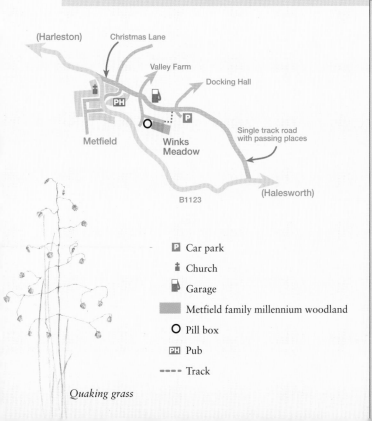

(Harleston)
Christmas Lane
Valley Farm
Docking Hall
PH
Metfield
Winks Meadow
Single track road with passing places
(Halesworth)
B1123

P Car park

🛉 Church

Garage

Metfield family millennium woodland

O Pill box

PH Pub

---- Track

Quaking grass

Map
OS Landranger 156

Grid reference
TM 306798

Size
1.4 hectares (3.5 acres)

Status
SSSI

Parking
At pull-in near road to Docking Hall

Local facilities
Metfield

Walking conditions
Mostly dry

Dogs
Sorry no dogs

Best time to visit
April–July

WORTHAM LING

"Walks in late summer among amethyst heath acquaint us with an exquisite medley of wildlife – all finely tuned to thrive in their specific surroundings."

This large tract of heathland near the River Waveney provides an interesting mix of habitats with an impressive variety of plants. Woodland and scrub, short acid grassland, heathland, ponds and chalky areas combine to provide a delightful selection of wildlife.

Look out for the erect, egg-yellow flowers of golden rod. In the small chalky areas you will find dwarf thistle, wild thyme and dropwort. In the damper hollows Devil's-bit scabious and tormentil occur. Butterflies are abundant in summer especially along the edges of hedgerows. Small copper, small heath and gatekeeper are very common and grayling and green hairstreak are present in good numbers. Heather, sheep's sorrel and gorse feature in the heathland areas along with occasional bee and pyramidal orchid. Plenty of fungi, mosses and lichen can also be seen here.

STAR SPECIES

Green woodpecker

Grayling butterfly

Golden rod

As Wortham Ling is a common, local people (the commoners) have rights to graze up to 200 sheep on the site but nowadays this simply doesn't happen. Without this traditional grazing the heath and grassland run the risk of being invaded by scrub. To conserve the open character of the area, chalk grassland is mown every year while most of the common is kept closely cropped by rabbit.

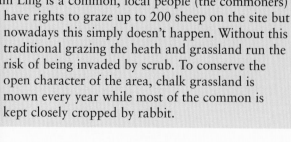

Grayling butterfly

Wortham Ling is cared for by Suffolk Wildlife Trust on behalf of the De Lancey & De la Hante Foundation.

Other Trust reserves nearby: Redgrave & Lopham Fen, Thelnetham Fen

This parasol mushroom has yet to open fully

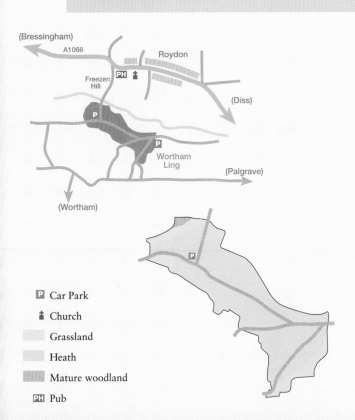

Map
OS Landranger 144

Grid reference
TM 088797

Size
51.5 hectares (128.75 acres)

Status
SSSI

Parking
Various, at Wortham Ling

Local facilities
Local pub

Walking conditions
Good but watch for holes

Dogs
On leads only

Best time to visit
April–Sept

P Car Park

✝ Church

Grassland

Heath

Mature woodland

PH Pub

BLYTHE MEADOW

STAR SPECIES
Lady's mantle

This grassland is an excellent example of unimproved meadow in a tranquil valley setting. It is the only site in Suffolk for lady's mantle – a plant with small greenish flowers and cloak-like leaves. The unusual mix of other wildflowers includes green-winged orchid, heath spotted orchid, moonwort fern, quaking grass and many sedges.

To conserve this lovely range of wild plants and flowers, the site is regularly grazed by cattle in summer.

Blythe Meadow is privately owned. For access please contact Suffolk Wildlife Trust.

Other Trust reserves nearby: The Mere, Framlingham

Map
OS Landranger 156

Grid reference
TM 323640

Size
4 hectares (10 acres)

Status
SSSI

Parking
On roadside at NW end of meadow

Local facilities
Framlingham

Walking conditions
Damp

Access
By prior arrangement

Dogs
On leads only

Best time to visit
May–June

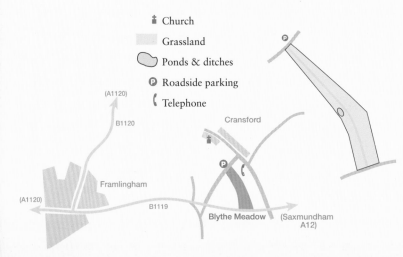

BRANDON ARTEMISIA

STAR SPECIES
Field wormwood
Sand catchfly

This pocket sized nature reserve on Brandon Industrial Estate,
supports the largest colony of field wormwood in Britain.
This rare plant has developed on the typically sandy soils of
Breckland and its unscented yellow flowers appear in August and
September. The seeds only germinate under special conditions
and this, combined with creeping urban development and
changes in agriculture, have contributed to its scarcity.

Look out for the pink flowers of sand catchfly,
a species almost completely restricted to Suffolk.
This little annual germinates in patches of open
ground in autumn and flowers in early summer.
Its tiny flowers are dwarfed by the large striped
seed pod which make it easy to spot. Other plants
to look out for are the nationally scarce bur
medick, smooth cat's-ear and bearded fescue.
Brandon Artemisia is leased to Suffolk Wildlife Trust
by Forest Heath District Council.

Other Trust reserves nearby:
Pashford Poors Fen, Wangford Warren

Sand catchfly

Map
OS Landranger 144

Grid reference
TL 773854

Size
0.1 hectares
(0.25 acres)

Status
SSSI

Parking
Roadside next
to reserve

Local facilities
Brandon

Walking conditions
Good

Dogs
Sorry no dogs,
sensitive site

Best time to visit
June, Aug, Sept

✝ Church

🅿 Roadside parking

FOX FRITILLARY MEADOW

STAR SPECIES

*Snake's head
fritillary*

The largest of four
remaining snake's head
fritillary sites in Suffolk,
this reserve is a fragment
of ancient meadow.
The plants thrive in a soil
that is waterlogged in winter and displays of up to 300,000
nodding purple-chequered and white heads in mid April and
early May are stunning.

*Snake's head
fritillary*

Eighteen fritillary sites were known in Suffolk in 1889, but sadly
most have been lost through drainage or ploughing.
The fritillaries bloom alongside meadow flowers such as
cowslip and cuckoo flower. In early July after the seeds
have set, the meadow is mown for hay and then grazed by
sheep. This helps to control vigorous grasses that would
otherwise smother the flowers.

The site gets its name from the Fox family who owned
Boundary Farm between 1922 and 1976 and helped
Suffolk Wildlife Trust buy the meadow. Visits can be
made during the annual Open Day in April, by kind
permission of the farm owners Mr & Mrs C Bacon.
Please contact Suffolk Wildlife Trust to visit at any
other time.

*Other Trust reserves nearby:
Martin's Meadows, Mickfield Meadow*

Map
OS Landranger 156

Grid reference
TM 187607

Size
2.4 hectares (6 acres)

Status
SSSI

Parking
By arrangement at
Boundary Farm on
A1120

Local facilities
Debenham, Earl Soh

Walking conditions
Can be wet

Access
Contact the Trust

Dogs
On leads only

Best time to visit
April open day

🕆 Chapel/Church

🅿 Parking

PH Pub

🗼 Windmill

REX GRAHAM RESERVE

STAR SPECIES

Military orchid

Mezereon

Adder's tongue

Military orchid

This small chalk pit lying deep within Thetford Forest has the largest colony of military orchid in Britain. In fact the reserve is named after the local botanist who discovered them. Other plants include heavily scented mezereon with its rosy-pink flowers, twayblade, pyramidal orchid and adder's tongue. Moonwort can be found in the network of rides in the surrounding forest together with a wide range of butterflies such as the orange tip and speckled wood.

Rex Graham is cared for by Suffolk Wildlife Trust on behalf of the Forestry Commission. Access on Bank Holiday Monday open day in late May or by contacting Suffolk Wildlife Trust.

Other reserves nearby: Lackford Lakes, Norah Hanbury-Kelk Meadows

Map
OS Landranger 143

Grid reference
TL 742747

Size
0.27 hectares (0.68 acres)

Status
SSSI, Natura 2000

Parking
Turn up ride 306 and park either side of gateway

Local facilities
Little Chef, Barton Mills roundabout

Walking conditions
Boardwalk/steep steps down to pit

Dogs
Sorry no dogs

Best time to visit
May Bank Holiday

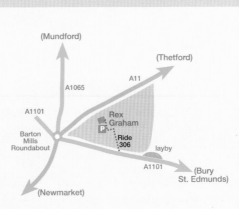

P Car park

Conifer plantation *Forest Enterprise*

.... Track

LOOKING TO THE FUTURE

From its early beginnings over 40 years ago, as a group of naturalists concerned about the damage to Redgrave and Lopham Fen, the Trust has become Suffolk's most dynamic and influential conservation organisation.

As it has matured, the Trust has retained the energy and urgency of the early days and turned it into a powerful advocate and guardian for Suffolk's wildlife.

With over 16000 members, support for the Trust has never been stronger and continues to rise. People are the key to the conservation of our wildlife and the growing interest in the protection of our natural heritage bodes well for the future.

The most significant decision you can make to safeguard the unique wildlife sites highlighted in this guide is to join the Trust.

If you are not already a member of the Trust, please call *01473 890089* today to find out more. Alternatively, you can join via our website at *www.wildlifetrust.org.uk/suffolk*

The diversity and extent of the Trust's work is only made possible through the commitment of over 1300 active volunteers who are involved in all areas of our work.

There are opportunities throughout the county to play an active part in the conservation of our reserves.

To find out more about how you can help, please call the Trust on *01473 890089*

Thank you for supporting Suffolk's wildlife.

Suffolk Wildlife Trust safeguards the wildlife and habitats of Suffolk for the future

Our work involves:

Caring for nature reserves

Advising on the management of other land

Protecting wildlife sites and threatened species

Educating and inspiring people of all ages

Campaigning on wildlife issues

Enabling people to take action for wildlife

Join us today and add your support to Suffolk's wildlife